CRE▲TIVE
HOMEOWNER®

design ideas for
Windows

CREATIVE HOMEOWNER®, Upper Saddle River, New Jersey

DESIGN IDEAS FOR WINDOWS

SENIOR EDITOR: Kathie Robitz
SENIOR DESIGNER: Glee Barre
GRAPHIC DESIGNER: Susan Johnston
EDITORIAL ASSISTANT: Jennifer Calvert (proofreading)
INDEXER: Schroeder Indexing Services
FRONT COVER PHOTOGRAPHY: (*top*) Mark Lohman; (*bottom left*) Mark Samu;
   (*bottom center*) Bill Rothschild; (*bottom right*) Mark Lohman
INSIDE FRONT COVER PHOTOGRAPHY: (*top*) courtesy of Hunter Douglas;
   (*bottom*) Paul Johnson, design: Austin Interiors
BACK COVER PHOTOGRAPHY: (*top*) Mark Lohman; (*bottom right*) Bob Greenspan;
   (*bottom center*) Mark Samu; (*bottom left*) Debbie Patterson/Prima U.K./Retna Ltd.
INSIDE BACK COVER PHOTOGRAPHY: courtesy of Hunter Douglas

CREATIVE HOMEOWNER

VP/EDITORIAL DIRECTOR: Timothy O. Bakke
PRODUCTION MANAGER: Kimberly H. Vivas
ART DIRECTOR: David Geer
MANAGING EDITOR: Fran J. Donegan

Printed in China

Current Printing (last digit)
10 9 8 7 6 5 4 3

Design Ideas for Windows, First Edition
Library of Congress Control Number: 2006931863
ISBN-10: 1-58011-334-6
ISBN-13: 978-1-58011-334-2

CREATIVE HOMEOWNER®
A Division of Federal Marketing Corp.
24 Park Way
Upper Saddle River, NJ 07458
www.creativehomeowner.com

Dedication

For Dennis, who helped every day.

Acknowledgments

My deepest gratitude goes to Kathie Robitz, who offered every kind of help and support throughout this project, with intelligence, tact, and good will. Thanks to Susan Johnston, who solved all difficulties with grace, style, and common sense. And thanks to all the photographers whose beautiful work made this book possible.

Contents

ABOVE Colorful fabric and practical grommets give contemporary draperies an informal, welcoming look.

RIGHT A sweetly scalloped festoon valance makes a soft, simple window dressing for a sunny breakfast nook.

BELOW Update traditional windows with tailored linen valances and blinds that have a modern air yet are true to the down-to earth attitude of American country style.

Any window treatment—from the simplest shade to the most elaborate arrangement of draperies—needs to fulfill both a functional and an aesthetic role in your decor. A beautiful design that makes your room too dark or fails to provide needed privacy will be unsatisfactory. Conversely, an awkwardly proportioned or skimpy treatment will never be pleasing, even if it works perfectly on a practical level. The infinite options in construction, materials, and styles can create confusion, leaving you feeling lost rather than empowered. This book will clear the confusion by leading you through the process of identifying

Introduction

and analyzing the issues of both form and function that apply to your own windows. It will enable you to narrow and focus on the range of choices that will suit your taste and practical needs. You'll find lots of help for identifying and refining your own sense of style, as well as "rules of thumb" for what works, helping you to avoid costly mistakes. The many beautiful examples of traditional and innovative designs will inspire your own selection of window treatments for your home.

The window treatment you choose for your room will affect how those who enter perceive the space and whether they feel comfortable in it. Is the overall look attractive and welcoming, or cold and forbidding? In this chapter, you will explore all the decisions necessary to narrow down the infinite choices to the one that's just right for your room and the way you want to live in it. Each decision will be quick, easy, and fun to make. At the end of the chapter, you'll have ruled out all the tempting but impractical distractions, ready to consider a well-edited short list of real possibilities.

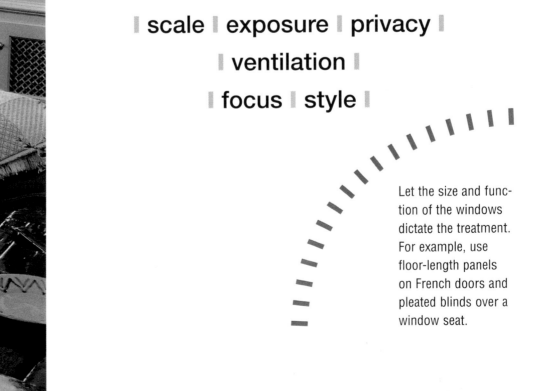

Versatility and Style

I scale I exposure I privacy I
I ventilation I
I focus I style I

Let the size and function of the windows dictate the treatment. For example, use floor-length panels on French doors and pleated blinds over a window seat.

Scale is the first element the eye discerns. Scale is a matter of size and also visual weight. When a window treatment's scale is wrong, it looks out of balance in the room, making you feel subtly ill at ease in the space. An elaborate, heavy treatment of multiple layers—shades, sheers, draperies, and valances—can look gracious and elegant if it's well proportioned to the windows and

scale

the size and style of the room, but in a small, simply furnished space it will be overwhelming. A lightweight café curtain is fresh and pretty on a kitchen window, but in a large family room filled with upholstered furniture, the same curtain will look skimpy and inadequate. In rooms furnished with large pieces, window treatments must be substantial—whether they are simple or extravagant in style—in order to balance the weight of the furniture. In addition, carpeted rooms call for weightier treatments than those with area rugs or bare floors.

simple and light

As a rule, keep the window treatments simple and light

▌ **in small rooms,** such as a tiny bedroom.

▌ **in rooms with many fixtures,** such as kitchens and baths.

▌ **in rooms with lots of built-in storage units,** such as home offices and kids' rooms.

▌ **in rooms that see heavy-duty use,** such as mudrooms, sunrooms, laundries, and entry halls.

OPPOSITE TOP Over a corner tub, tailored bamboo blinds control light and privacy but add little bulk.

OPPOSITE Light, easily laundered café curtains are a low-maintenance solution for a busy mudroom and provide just enough privacy.

ABOVE The large windows in this generously proportioned bedroom can take an elaborate, weighty treatment of gathered balloon shades, floor-length panels, and shaped and gathered valances.

bright idea

distract the eye

If the view's a little bleak but you need to maximize light, try a sheer, fanciful treatment: hang transparent ribbons from a tension rod and glue a silk bloom, a button, or other small ornament onto the bottom of each to add a bit of weight.

ABOVE Half-length wooden shutters provide privacy and light control, making this kitchen corner both bright and cozy. Fabric valances soften the look.

Exposure is all about how open the room should be to the outside world. The view is the first thing you notice, and if it's the neighbor's garbage cans or something equally uninspiring, you'll want to screen it. You can do that with sheers—fabric panels or blinds—that will admit plenty of light, or with slats— shutters or blinds—that will give you less light but more air. In a cool climate, sheers make more sense; in a hot one, slats are more appealing. Screening the view may call for covering only part of the window. If the top shows only trees and sky, you can consider a café curtain or a blind that draws up from the bottom.

exposure

ABOVE Bright-colored sheers add a brilliant glow to a room. Tucking the fabric gives the effect of translucent stripes that increase privacy without significantly reducing light.

RIGHT Sheer panels can be drawn back to showcase a dramatic view or closed to soften too-bright sunlight.

BELOW Multiple layers of sheer and opaque panels protect this quiet alcove from the elements while admitting plenty of light for reading.

RIGHT A versatile combination of simple matchstick blinds and easily drawn panels suspended from rings allows for quick response to changes in light and temperature.

E ven if the view is pleasant, the light coming in may be too strong. In cool climates or seasons, sheers or slats will diffuse the light. But if it's hot, you may want to exclude as much sun as possible to keep down the air-conditioning bill. You can do this with lined draperies or with multiple layers, such as a sheer blind topped with a panel that you can draw over the window during temperature extremes.

IIII protection from the elements IIIIIIIIIIIIIIIIIIIIIIIIIII

muffle sound

Layering is also your first defense against unwanted noise, whether it's from traffic or neighbors' outdoor activities. Fabric treatments muffle noise more effectively than those constructed of hard materials, such as wooden shutters or metal blinds. Also,

I **line** draperies and curtains.

I **add an interlining**—a third layer of fabric between the face fabric and the lining.

I **choose deeply pleated headings** to increase fabric fullness.

LEFT Softly gathered blinds in crisp white soften light without darkening the room. The patterned, scalloped valance is feminine without looking too fussy.

BELOW Tailored fabric blinds topped with lined, floor-length panels form a double layer of protection against cold drafts yet easily open to let the sunshine inside.

stay warm

The same layering and covering solutions that keep you cooler in hot weather will insulate against heat loss in cold. Boost the comfort of your room by choosing a window treatment that opens to admit as much precious winter sun as possible and closes to exclude drafts and reduce heat loss on cold nights.

privacy

The view, light, air, heat, and sound that come into your home are mirrored by those same elements that your windows emit. You can best check the view into your room by turning on all the lights after dark and asking another person to move around the space while you go outside and look. Baths and bedrooms demand complete privacy, and a sheer panel or bamboo blind that suffices during the day will not do the job at night. On the other hand, you may not mind if a dog-walking neighbor can see you at the kitchen sink or watching TV in the family room. But if you feel too visible in any room, you'll need to correct the situation. This can be as simple as installing an opaque roller shade behind a light curtain.

LEFT Lined-fabric blinds can add color and pattern while affording complete privacy when needed. Even a bathroom facing a private yard can feel uncomfortably exposed after dark.

OPPOSITE TOP These panels are stationary, so venetian blinds behind the sheers are essential for nighttime privacy.

OPPOSITE BOTTOM These dramatically draped panels hang from rosettes and do not close. There's no real need for privacy in this room, but a large indoor tree provides a sense of shelter.

bright idea

green screen

Even a large plant can serve as a window "treatment" to partially obscure the view into your living room.

The traditional rule has been that there be uniformity of all windows in style and color as seen from the street. Many designers now dismiss this idea as old fashioned, impractical, and limiting. For example, if there are formal draperies in a front room that's on the right side of your house, you can still use an informal treatment, such as bamboo blinds, in the room on the left side.

the view from outside

On the other hand, if your home is traditional in style and visible as a whole from the street (not screened by trees and shrubbery), you may prefer to adhere to the old rule.

ABOVE The windows here look balanced because the window treatments, although different, cover only the lower half of both windows.

OPPOSITE The windows in this home look symmetrical on the outside because the curtains' lining and tieback height are identical in every case.

present a **u**niform **f**acade

You can vary your window treatments from room to room and keep the view from the street similar with any of these choices:

▮ **Panels with identical, neutral linings**. Change the face fabrics to match the decor of each room.

▮ **Identical sheer, neutral curtains or blinds**. Add any treatment you like on top, as the sheers will be the only thing that shows from outside.

▮ **A versatile neutral option**. Wooden shutters, classic blinds, or Roman shades look good in any room. Subtle color changes—white, beige, taupe, gray—won't be perceptible from the street.

ABOVE Lace panels, gathered on rods at both the top and bottom, allow French doors to open easily.

OPPOSITE TOP A hinged rod swings to the side, allowing a round casement window to open wide.

OPPOSITE LEFT Shutters that fold flat against the wall can be a convenient solution for both protecting and exposing awkwardly placed windows.

OPPOSITE RIGHT Consider using a pretty top treatment combined with simple blinds to soften and dress a variety of windows without interfering with their operation.

ventilation

Fresh air is extremely important in every room. Recent studies show that outdoor air is invariably cleaner than indoor air. Heating, cooling, cooking, and washing dishes and laundry all produce air pollution, not to mention the contaminants emitted by paint, carpeting, plastics, and other materials. You should ventilate your home in mild weather, unless it's prohibited by special allergies. All window treatments should allow for easy access to outdoor air, even if their function is for privacy or insulation.

|| welcome a breeze to clean the air in your home ||||||||||||

window **t**reatment **w**orksheet

With this table you can easily choose a treatment to suit your needs.

	lightweight curtains	lined draperies	opaque fabric shades	sheer fabric blinds	shutters	woven wood shades	slatted blinds	top treatments
large scale	no	yes	yes	yes	yes	yes	yes	yes
small scale	yes	no	yes	yes	yes	yes	yes	yes
frame view	yes	yes	no	no	yes	no	no	yes
soften view	yes	no	no	yes	no	no	no	no
block view	no	yes	yes	no	yes	yes	yes	no
diffuse light	yes	no	no	yes	no	yes	yes	no
block light	no	yes	yes	no	yes	no	yes	no
reduce sound	no	yes	yes	yes	yes	no	yes	no
daytime privacy	yes	yes	yes	yes	yes	yes	yes	no
nighttime privacy	no	yes	yes	no	yes	no	yes	no
insulate	no	yes	yes	no	yes	no	yes	no

OPPOSITE LEFT These shutters swing easily on hinges to cover or expose a window, and the louvers open and close, allowing you to filter light and ventilation.

OPPOSITE RIGHT Blinds that open from top and bottom make it easy to fine-tune the light level and the view, while heavy draperies can be drawn closed to exclude the outside world completely.

ABOVE This traditional combination of sheer panels and lined draperies has been time-tested for comfort and versatility.

Any window is an important architectural and functional element in a room: it occupies prime vertical space, and is your "eye" on the world. But how important a window *looks* has little to do with its size; it's all about emphasis. How much or how little depends on you. A little orange café curtain in an all-white powder room draws attention. Change that little curtain to white, and put a vase of hot-pink peonies on the vanity—and now where does your eye go? Keep this basic rule in mind: there can be only one main focal point in a room. Modern and contemporary styles dictate that, in addition, there may also be up to two lesser focal points. Traditional styles are more diffuse; besides the main focal point, there may be several secondary focal points and any number of smaller supplemental spots of interest, depending on the size of the room. Remember: less is more in small rooms.

windows as focal points

OPPOSITE The four-poster is the main focal point in this serene bedroom, and a wall covered with floor-length draperies in a subtle blue-gray fabric provides a perfect backdrop for it.

ABOVE By virtue of size and placement, the upholstered bed is again the main focal point. But in this traditionally styled room, the flowered fabric, pretty trim, and elaborately draped valances ensure that the windows get their share of attention.

bright idea

big spaces

In open-plan or great rooms, different areas can be treated as separate units in terms of a focal point, although common elements such as wall color, flooring, and fabrics should unite the whole space.

ABOVE AND LEFT Matching draperies and hardware tie the living and dining areas of this great room together. They're simple enough to keep the focus on the fireplace and the table.

OPPOSITE Golden silk draperies with detailed cornices draw attention to the tall, beautiful windows in this room.

working with focal points

ABOVE The rich, yet subtle, coloring of these traditional window treatments blends with the paneled walls to keep the focus on the fireplace and the gilt-framed painting above it.

play down the windows

Don't let your window treatments compete with these focal points:

▎ A fireplace

▎ A large TV

▎ A kitchen island topped with a pot rack

▎ An important painting

▎ A canopy, four-poster, or otherwise elaborate bed

play **u**p the **w**indows

Give star billing to windows that earn the spotlight:

▎ Large windows with beautiful proportions

▎ Any window with a great view

▎ French or sliding glass doors

▎ A bay or bow window

▎ Any window that admits especially lovely light

ABOVE The scalloped and swagged valance dramatizes this handsome wall of windows, and the furniture placement, with the sofa centered in front of them, reinforces their importance. Note how the scalloped valance echoes the curves of the coffee table.

LEFT A beautiful, artfully placed chaise focuses attention on the bare windows and their view, while floor-to-ceiling louvered shutters become part of the architecture of the room and obscure a less attractive view.

modern style

I f your style is modern or contemporary and you've already chosen another main focal point, the windows become part of the "shell" of the room; they become part of the background, blending into the walls and allowing the star element to shine. You can choose from simple fabric draperies; blinds made of paper, fabric, wood, or metal; or no treatment, leaving the windows bare, depending on your functional needs and the scale you've determined. The color should match in hue or tone (intensity) with the surrounding walls for a clean, seamless look.

If your windows are the focal point in a modern setting, the treatment should be clean and simple, but there should be something about it that draws the eye. You could use brilliant color in an otherwise neutral setting. You might frame the windows with a pared-down, deconstructed version of a traditional treatment, such as a swag. Or you could simply make the windows the focus of the room by your arrangement of the furniture and artwork.

FAR LEFT Simple panels and blinds blend into the background to keep the focus on the stunning fireplace.

LEFT The clean lines of a pleated blind keep the look modern, while the bright blue color, in an otherwise neutral setting, draws the eye to the window.

BELOW Sliding shoji screens are an elegant, understated way to focus attention on the windows. Note that the clerestory windows have been left bare for an uncluttered look.

ABOVE Here the window draperies are the focus of the room. The strong color contrast, elaborate valances, and luxurious trims all contribute to their importance.

LEFT No single element stands out here. The patterned and draped windows, fine paneling, antique chest, and unusual accessories unite into a seamless whole.

RIGHT Pretty fabric, draping, and trim make the windows important, but they're well balanced by patterns and piping on the furniture and a pleasant clutter of accessories.

FAR RIGHT Keep a window treatment in balance, despite a generous use of fabric, pattern, and detail, by making the coloring more muted than the other elements of the decor.

When your style is any of the myriad traditional ones—or an eclectic combination of several—you may be less inclined to make the windows the main focal point because you probably already chose something else, such as a fireplace. But you may call upon the windows to act as a secondary focal point or third-level spot of interest. If that is the case, downplay the window treatment but balance the room by adding substance and detail, perhaps with hardware, that will link the windows visually or thematically to the main focal point.

traditional style

FAR LEFT Add a traditional touch to any room with a valance. Using high-contrast colors, patterns, and trims will draw attention to the window.

LEFT In a simple transition space, such as a hallway or entry, an elaborate window or door treatment will provide the only focal point needed.

All traditional and period-inspired styles—from fringed, tasseled, and swagged Victorian to simple Shaker curtains gathered on a string—have details specific to them. How authentic you want to be is up to you, but the modern take is to give a nod to tradition but to simplify it. This is especially true if your windows beg to be showcased because of their great view or surrounding woodwork. For instance, in a Regency-style bedroom, you might choose a simple draped-fabric valance for the window, with a fabric shade that you can pull down for privacy, forgoing the floor-sweeping panels that are usually part of that decorative period.

LEFT Sheer fabric is puffed and tied invisibly into a traditional form and left untrimmed, giving a romantic style a more relaxed, contemporary look.

ABOVE Highlight a simple panel with a beautifully detailed tasseled tieback for a luxurious look.

bright idea
time travel

You can also use window treatments to transform a room with no particular style into a fantasy of another place and time.

period details

ABOVE LEFT A substantial pole finished with a handsome finial, deep fringe, thick cords, and large tassels add weight to this Regency-style drapery.

LEFT Emphasize the scalloped edge of a balloon shade with interesting fringe.

BOTTOM FAR LEFT A shaped and swagged valance looks more finished with a trimmed edge.

BOTTOM LEFT This simple pleated blind would look modern if left untrimmed and made in a solid color. It's the fringe and the printed fabric that give it period style.

color,

quick, colorful changes

Be creative in small informal rooms using treatments that are easy, fast, and fun!

1 **Screw rosette holdbacks** into the top corners of a window frame, and drape a hemmed length of fabric over them.

2 **Stretch a length of clothesline** across a window; attach dishtowels with clothespins. It's cute in a laundry room.

3 **String, thumbtacks, clothespins,** and maybe a tension rod are all the low-tech tools you need to create a pretty window covering from vintage fabrics.

4 **Loop ribbon** between two hooks at the top of a window. Fold a fabric panel over the upper strand; bring the panel over the lower strand; and pleat it to the desired depth.

pattern, and texture

Window treatments give you an opportunity to add color, pattern, and texture to a room. This is especially easy to do and attractive in rooms where inexpensive ready-mades or your own sewing skills are sufficient to dress the windows.

ABOVE Even if you don't sew, it's easy to use fusible webbing to hem all four sides of a length of fabric to make a panel. Hand-sew or clip rings to the top edge for hanging.

RIGHT Stitching hems and a rod pocket into fabric lengths is an easy sewing project. Use the remnants to make cushion covers, and you have a whole new look.

BELOW Tone-on-tone pattern and rich warm colors that echo the wood tones in the room make draperies that are easy to live with but far from bland.

RIGHT This pale, neutral print will allow the homeowner to introduce changes in color in the bedding and other elements of the room.

FAR RIGHT A subtle tonal pattern that reads more as a texture than as a print enriches these draperies.

conservative choices

In rooms where the windows necessitate custom-made treatments, possibly involving many yards of expensive fabric, you'll naturally gravitate toward more conservative choices to prevent an expensive mistake. However, the conservative choice doesn't preclude using color, texture, or pattern to enrich your room. Let's say you've decided that a simple cream-colored curtain panel to blend with the cream-colored walls will function best in the space you're decorating. You still have the option of using a tone-on-tone vertical-stripe damask, which will not only add texture and pattern but make the ceiling look higher.

bright idea
subtle touch
Choose a contrasting lining fabric to add texture, substance, and a hint of color when the draperies are pulled back.

ABOVE Beautifully upholstered and piped cornices and a geometric print fabric enhance classic draperies in a room with a soothing color scheme.

LEFT Choose neutral colors when you want to introduce pattern into a room without disrupting a subtle or serene look.

LEFT Horizontal stripes will help prevent tall windows and a high ceiling from seeming overly imposing. Coordinating the colors of the draperies with the furniture will help unite the large vertical expanse with the living space.

S triped fabrics work decorating magic. Running vertically (the usual direction), they increase the apparent height of the windows and the ceiling. You can increase the illusion of height by mounting the window treatments above the window—even just under the ceiling—and making them floor length. Horizontal stripes make windows look wider and inject a modern or Asian sensibility. Gathering, pleating, and draping stripes gives the room a quality of movement and grace, while using them flat brings a sense of stability and control.

LEFT Use vertical stripes to break up a wide wall of windows. The informal draping and patterning of this fabric soften the geometry of the room.

BELOW LEFT Here, narrow stripes used flat look crisp and controlled—in keeping with the strict geometry of the built-in bookcases.

BELOW CENTER A soft color contrast in vertical stripes "heightens" the windows and "lifts" the ceiling without drawing undue attention to the visual trickery in play.

BELOW RIGHT Pleating, gathering, and changing the direction of stripes will accentuate the forms of a window treatment and distinguish the vertical, horizontal, and accenting elements from one another.

the magic of stripes

LEFT A muted color scheme and a simple self-valance design give these curtains a comfortable, always-been-there look that's not too feminine for any room.

BELOW A wide band of solid fabric contains a sinuous pattern and imparts a tailored air to these draperies.

FAR LEFT Add ruffled edges, a gathered valance, and a draped tieback to take flowered curtains to the maximum level of frilliness.

LEFT Update chintz by choosing a foliage pattern in muted colors and making it into a simple, untrimmed pleated blind.

BELOW In another way to modernize chintz, a bright red background color brings a relaxed country air to the room.

cheerful chintz

C hintz refers to a glazing process that gives this perennial favorite fabric its satiny sheen, but it has also come to refer to exuberant flowery patterns. Not all chintzes are floral, however; foliage, birds, and scenic patterns are other popular themes. Using these patterns is a sure way to inject your room with warmth and charm, as they always suggest a comfortable, English country house atmosphere. Use them in generous swathes—pleating, gathering, and draping them—for a feminine look. Or, if that's too fussy for your taste, handle them in a simple, understated way for a more subtle nod to tradition. Tip: washing strips the polish from the fabric; to retain the sheen, always dry-clean chintz draperies.

▮▮ balancing patterns ▮▮▮▮▮▮▮▮▮▮▮▮▮▮▮▮▮▮▮▮

I f there is already pattern in a room, on the walls, floor, or furniture, you should definitely consider adding more with the window treatment. Multiple patterns balance each other. The secret to making this work is to change the scale. For example, a large-flowered chintz on the sofa will look great with a narrow stripe on the curtains and a medium plaid on side chairs. Just be sure to use patterns that have some colors in common. Another idea: choose a bold print or a strongly contrasting color for window treatments to make them the center of attention, especially in a room filled with solid, neutral fabrics.

bright idea

smart shopping

When you're trying to balance a lot of colors and patterns, swatches are a great help. Collect paint chips and fabric samples in a notebook for easy reference.

LEFT A mix of well-balanced patterns creates a cheerful look. The narrow stripe on the curtain fabric would fade into invisibility were it not for the boldly striped banding and the multi-colored, tasseled trim.

▮
ABOVE LEFT Change of scale and related colors are what make mixed patterns look as if they belong together.

▮
ABOVE Four or five patterns aren't too many, as long as the colors relate. The more patterns you include, the more closely the colors should match.

Now that you have identified how your window treatments should function and have begun to explore your style options, it's time to consider practicalities. You'll need to think through the architecture of your windows, their proportions, and placement. Maintenance and budget matters are more flexible, and here you'll find ideas for easy care and ways to keep costs down by developing an expensive treatment in manageable steps over time. Correct measurements and hardware are important, too. Will you do all of this yourself or seek professional help? Read on and explore the possibilities.

Planning

I architecture I window types I
I size and proportion I maintenance I
I budget I measuring I hardware I
I hiring a pro I

A substantial pole supports a graceful swag, giving an air of formality to this sunroom, while louvered blinds control light and privacy.

To start, you'll need to evaluate your windows' assets or drawbacks. Are they framed in woodwork? If so, is it really special, moderately attractive, or best concealed? How do the windows fit in with the room's architectural elements, such as the doors, baseboard and crown moldings, built-ins, or other permanent features?

working with the architecture

OPPOSITE Floor-length draperies are suspended from beneath a wooden cornice to highlight the beautiful woodwork.

ABOVE Create a traditional effect in a modern home by obscuring the woodwork. Here, outside-mounted bamboo blinds and generous draperies cover the window surrounds. Using a strong pattern on both walls and windows reinforces the illusion.

RIGHT Informal translucent panels cover modern windows completely in a romantic bedroom.

f windows have good "bones"—whether authentically period, lovingly restored, or well-designed new construction—and if the architectural elements of the room fit together seamlessly, you may dress them simply or elaborately. There's no need to worry about camouflage or optical illusions when planning the window treatments.

▐ ▐ ▐ ▐ ▐ revealing ideas ▐ ▐ ▐ ▐ ▐ ▐ ▐ ▐ ▐ ▐ ▐ ▐ ▐ ▐ ▐ ▐ ▐ ▐

ABOVE A simple blind on the window allows the arched form of the enclosure to take the spotlight.

LEFT TOP Pretty 12-over-12 mullioned windows are highlighted with a sunny-color paint treatment and wooden half-shutters.

LEFT BOTTOM Hang draperies so that they stack back on the walls to reveal elegantly detailed, arched windows.

ABOVE A swagged sheer treatment softens modern windows and connects them to the traditional elements of the decor without detracting from their dramatic proportions.

OPPOSITE Make a small window look larger and more important with a top treatment that hangs from just below the ceiling line and panels that extend slightly beyond the window frame, leaving most of the glass exposed.

LEFT The bold pattern on these roller shades attracts the eye and disguises the reality of three different window sizes in this charming remodeled kitchen in an older home.

BELOW Waterfall draping provides soft vertical folds that give a taller, more gracious look to short windows.

concealing ideas

Sometimes, rooms have been remodeled in such a way that the windows are out of character with the rest of the space. For example, in an older home, an updated room or an addition with large picture windows or glass doors may benefit from the amount of sunlight they admit, but the windows may look out of place with the earlier construction. Windows in a single room may vary widely in size, shape, and placement. Some may be traditionally framed while others may have no trim at all. Here, your challenge is to balance the new and old windows, and use optical illusions to create a uniform look.

window types

Windows are categorized both by how they operate and by their style; within each category there are traditional and modern types. The photos here will help you identify window styles that may be in or out of character with the architecture in your house.

RIGHT The corner-spanning arrangement of these casement windows gives them a modern look. The soft fabric shades, which can be lowered if desired, will not interfere with opening or closing the units.

BELOW A custom-built wooden surround incorporates a fan-detailed cornice and louvered shutters to architectural importance to a bank of plain windows.

LEFT Double-hung windows are the most common type found in both old and new construction. The division of the window into small panes by mullions is more traditional in style.

LEFT BELOW French doors need a window treatment that won't interfere with their operation. Here, the draperies hang from an arched enclosure that lets the doors swing freely.

BELOW Track windows and, in this case, doors don't require any clearance to open, so you're free to dress them with draperies and blinds as you please.

LEFT A draped and pleated valance and floor-length panels are traditional treatments for double-hung windows.

BELOW Hang panels high from freely sliding rings to provide easy clearance for opening French doors.

RIGHT Casement windows swing outward and present no special problems. Make sure your draperies allow easy access to the cranks.

many window types ||||||||||||||||||||||||||||||||||||||||

most **p**opular

Double-hung window. This type of window has an upper and a lower sash that slide up and down to open and close. The glass may or may not be divided by mullions.

Casement window. Operated by turning a crank, a casement window is hinged vertically to swing out to open and in to close. The glass may or may not be divided by mullions.

French door. A glass pane, which may or may not be divided by mullions, extends the full length of a French door. A pair of French doors often takes the place of a large window.

bright idea

go with the flow

Track windows are best matched with vertical blinds that slide in the same direction.

RIGHT You can fit fixed windows with blinds that draw from both top and bottom to provide precise light control and privacy. In this bath, a ceiling exhaust provides ventilation.

BELOW Jalousie windows present no special problems in window dressing other than the need to allow access to the cranks.

what works for you?

more types

Fixed window. A nonoperable unit, it may be part of a larger window.

Slider. A window or glass door that has a top and bottom track on which the sash or door move sideways.

Awning window. A horizontally hinged window, it swings in or out.

Jalousie window. This window type has operable glass louvers.

ABOVE Vertical blinds are available in many styles and materials to provide a range of light control and privacy options for doors and windows that slide on tracks.

traditional styles

Bay and bow windows. Composed of multiple window frames these windows project beyond the exterior wall to form an alcove within the room. A bay is angled, a bow, curved. Either may enclose a window seat.

Palladian window. Strictly speaking, this is a symmetrical arrangement of three units—two narrow rectangular units flanking a wider, arched center unit—derived from designs by the sixteenth-century Italian architect, Palladio. There are many variations in modern construction that have been inspired by this style.

Fanlight. A semicircular (fan-shaped) window, it is usually above a window or door.

Sidelights. Usually fixed, these narrow glass units are arranged next to a larger window or a door.

Cameo window. This small oval, round, or octagonal window is usually fixed.

||||||||| highlight classic windows |||||||||||||||||

FAR LEFT This pretty octagonal leaded-glass cameo window admits extra light into a kitchen.

LEFT A stained-glass fanlight tops a window dressed with a simple fabric blind.

ABOVE Treat classically inspired windows very simply to maximize their grace and good looks.

ABOVE You can give a pared-down informal look to a bay window with sill-length panels on the sidelights, as in this room.

LEFT Fabric blinds dress the sidelights, framing the undressed center window to focus attention on the leaded-glass transom.

ABOVE A picture window is treated in typical mid-century modern style with tailored panels and no top treatment.

RIGHT Short, tailored valances highlight these windows located high on a stair wall.

work with the room's architecture

modern styles

Picture window. A large, fixed window, usually wider than tall, intended to frame a view and often flanked on each side by narrow units.

Clerestory window. A small narrow window set high on the wall, sometimes on an angle, and often part of a grouping. It may be fixed or operable.

Cathedral window. In a room with a vaulted ceiling, a large window, often topped with triangular or trapezoidal glass units, designed to follow the slope of the ceiling.

bright idea
artful geometry

Maintain the clean lines of modern architecture with straight-falling panels and simple blinds.

ABOVE A pleated blind and long draperies on the lower windows were combined on this cathedral window for versatile insulation, privacy, and light control. The upper portion of the window has been left bare to flood the room with a controlled amount of sunlight.

size and proportion

Window treatments can do a lot to change the apparent size of your windows, making them seem larger or smaller and balancing an odd assortment of sizes and shapes to produce a more coherent effect. Your eye will register the size and shape of the treatment rather than those of the window.

ABOVE Use two poles that connect with a matching "elbow" to unite two corner windows.

ABOVE RIGHT Tenting dormer windows provides a canopy effect for twin beds, while pleated blinds uniformly furnish all of the windows in the room.

RIGHT Covered with neutral shutters, the small window fades into the background here, allowing the generously draped glass doors to take center stage.

ABOVE Elegant lime-green silk taffeta curtains extend beyond the trim of this pair of French doors, both allowing the doors to open easily into the room and visually expanding the narrow space.

LEFT This bedroom window is a classic example of how to hang curtains to admit maximum light; very little of the glass is covered.

BELOW LEFT These upholstered cornices have been installed just under the ceiling to make the short windows appear taller.

ABOVE Treating two windows with a single blind is a way to make two small windows look like one larger opening.

RIGHT Translucent draperies, hung high and wide, turn small windows into a backdrop for a pretty bed.

windows too small?

Dealing with small windows is a common problem in older homes, built when glass was expensive and the double-glazing that prevents heat loss didn't exist. Getting enough natural light into the room is a related problem. These solutions address both issues:

▮ **Position the hardware** so that your window treatment hangs well above the window trim. Your windows will appear taller, and if you tie back the draperies, more of the glass will be exposed.

▮ **Install long curtain poles** so that, when the panels are drawn back, most of the glass is uncovered and the draperies can be stacked against the wall on either side of the window. Your windows will look wider and will admit maximum light.

▮ **Choose draperies** that reach to or puddle on the floor to make windows seem taller.

▮ **Treat multiple, consecutive units** on a wall with panels or blinds that sweep across all of them to give the impression of one expansive window.

windows too large?

Extra-large windows, a popular feature in new and remodeled homes today, can be dramatic. But they can also appear out of proportion and much too big on some older structures. It's not as easy to make a window look smaller as it is to visually increase its size, but there are some things you can do. Here are some examples:

▐ **Obliterate the problem** by covering the entire window wall with floor-to-ceiling draperies. This is an expensive solution (all that fabric!), but one that works equally well in traditional or modern interiors. Be sure to choose hardware that allows you to draw the draperies for light and ventilation, as desired.

▐ **Mount sheer fabric blinds** that cover the window while allowing light to enter. Match the blinds to the wall color, and the size and shape of the windows will seem to disappear.

▐ **Break up the window expanse** with a group of narrow blinds or shades that can be raised and lowered independently, or use panels that partially "cut" the window's width. This "divide and conquer" approach is the most versatile solution of all.

OPPOSITE FAR LEFT Use panels to cover the side windows if you wish to decrease the apparent width of a wall of windows.

OPPOSITE NEAR LEFT A large bay window is a pretty feature but it can be difficult to arrange furniture in front of it. Use floor-length panels to partially hide the window and create a backdrop for a seating arrangement.

ABOVE The band of rings that separates the upper flat panels from the lower gathered ones cuts the height of these windows and coordinates with the color of some of the cushions.

LEFT To smooth over the problem of varying sill heights, dress the windows with floor-length draperies.

BELOW Use valances hung from beneath the crown molding to camou-flage windows of different heights.

RIGHT Use draperies hung wide to balance a small window with a wide one and keep all the materials and hardware uniform.

BELOW RIGHT When the ceiling height varies from wall to wall, hang draperies equidistant from the top of the wall.

What if your room has vastly different windows—a big picture window with sidelights on one wall and a double-hung unit on another? Maybe you have a major Palladian or cathedral window in the same room with a strip of clerestories and a medium-size double-hung on another wall. What to do? The good news is that you don't need to treat all windows in the room alike. You can use a big treatment, such as draperies, on the big windows, and some-thing simpler, such as a Roman blind in a matching fabric, on the smaller ones. The attention you pay to finishing details will tie things together; if the draperies are trimmed with fringe, choose a similar, narrower fringe to edge the blind. And some windows, such as clerestories, don't need to be dressed at all.

dealing with multiple sizes and shapes

ABOVE With double-glazed windows facing a private woodland, there was no reason to cover these beautiful windows.

LEFT With the fanlights of a window open to the sun and stars, shutters provide privacy.

ABOVE RIGHT Leaded glass windows are too pretty to cover.

RIGHT A swagged treatment breaks the height of this grand window arrangement and conceals blinds that are pulled down at night to make the room feel cozy and private.

windows to leave bare

All the following windows, installed for light rather than privacy, can be left unadorned unless you have a definite need to exclude hot sun or cold air. This includes the arched or triangular windows that top Palladian or cathedral windows, whether or not you choose to dress the lower main window:

▮ fanlights ▮ sidelights ▮ cameos ▮ clerestories

using mock-ups

When you've got a look in mind but you're not sure how it will pan out, try a mockup. It will give you a good idea of how the size, shape, and scope of any window treatment will actually look in your room. Start with a photo or sketch of the style you're considering.

Here's what you'll need:

▐ **large pieces of fabric**—bed sheets or even a tarp

▐ **tape**—packing, duct, or masking tape

▐ **pins**—T-pins are best, but any type will do

▐ **string**—any type

Here's what to do:

1 **Clear the windows,** but leave the rest of the room intact—you'll want to judge your design in the context of the furnished room.

2 **Use tape to adhere the fabric** above and around the window in your planned design. Fold and pleat the fabric as necessary to approximate the finished size and shape you have in mind.

3 **Use pins and string to refine and shape** your creation, draping, tying, hemming, and poufing as needed.

4 **Leave it all in place** for a few days so you can judge the effect at different times of day with a fresh eye.

▐▐▐ playing with proportions ▐

OPPOSITE TOP Mocking up a blind will help you decide whether to use an inside mount or an outside mount, as shown.

OPPOSITE BOTTOM It makes sense to judge the effects of multiple elements—a padded cornice, puffed valance, pleated jabots, and Roman blinds—before cutting into expensive fabric.

ABOVE Judging the right depth of a cornice or valance can be tricky because there are so many variables in any situation. Adjust your mock-up until the proportions look just right.

LEFT Splashes and cooking odors are no problem with easily laundered cotton café curtains.

BELOW LEFT Choose plastic blinds for the lowest possible maintenance in a busy bath; they're quickly cleaned with a dip in the tub.

This can be a major issue in heavily used rooms or a minor one in rooms that are used lightly. Time and money are both important considerations. Elaborate draperies can be practical in a formal room that's used infrequently for entertaining and is off-limits to pets and small children. In such an instance, monthly vacuuming will be sufficient, and expensive, time-consuming dry cleaning may be necessary only every three years or so. The same treatment would be a nightmare in a family room, or even a master bedroom where children and pets are welcome visitors.

care and maintenance

Dusting and vacuuming are quick and easy cleaning methods, but be aware that it takes more time to dust intricate surfaces with lots of nooks and crannies. Removing, laundering, and rehanging is quick with simple curtains and valances, but a much bigger job if the fabric requires ironing, especially if there are ruffles, pleats, or tucks. Dry cleaning is the most costly form of maintenance, especially if the size of the treatment calls for professional removal and remounting.

LEFT MIDDLE Choose a simple style and an easy-care fabric for white curtains that keep their pristine looks.

LEFT Vacuum bamboo blinds with a brush attachment weekly to rid them of dust.

There are a few things to think about when you visualize actually living with a specific window treatment.

Kids like to play. Their games may easily involve turning long curtains into impromptu tents and hiding places. And even if your children confine their snacks and drinks to the kitchen or playroom, their friends may not. Most people with small children prefer to make the entire house at least somewhat kid-friendly, avoiding delicate silks and priceless brocades.

Pets enrich our lives in many ways, but they can be hard on furnishings. Floor-length curtains attract and hold hair; puddled draperies invite nesting; and a litter of kittens may turn any curtain into ribbons or a stringy mess of snagged and pulled threads. If animals are important in your heart and your home, avoid grief by choosing sill-length curtains in smooth, sturdy fabrics, hard-surfaced blinds, or louvered shutters.

allergies

Dust mites and pollen are common triggers of allergies. If a family member is afflicted

- **Keep window treatments** simple so you can vacuum and launder them easily and often.

- **Avoid lined-fabric** constructions that you must dry clean.

- **Use sheer panels** topped by separate unlined cotton panels, so both layers are easy to wash.

- **Choose hard-surfaced** blinds or shutters that are easy to dust or wipe down.

LEFT Fasten blind cords well out of reach, or choose blinds without cords, for safety in rooms for small children.

BELOW In a pet-friendly family room, simple fabric blinds dress the windows.

keeping things clean, safe, and user-friendly

OPPOSITE BOTTOM Shutters are easy to dust with the brush attachment of your vacuum cleaner, and they don't create dust as fabrics do.

OPPOSITE TOP Valances and roller shades are up and out of harm's way in a child's room.

IIII keeping things clean, safe, and user-friendly IIIIIIIIIII

irty air can arrive from outdoors or be created right at home by our own activities, especially cooking. How dirty the air is will certainly vary from room to room, and from season to season. Choose from easily cleaned options when planning window treatments for rooms that don't pass the clean-air test, such as your kitchen or any room that faces a busy street.

Odors are often related to dirty air, and cooking is the most common cause. But dampness can create musty smells. Generally, if odors are an issue, you need to solve it with a ventilation system or a dehumidifier. Also, don't allow your window treatment to compound the problem by impeding the exchange of stale and fresh air.

bright idea

physical impairments

Physical impairments take many forms and include the general frailty of old age. Some treatments may actually be dangerous because of extreme weight and others impractical for anyone confined to a wheelchair. Consider installing remote-controlled mechanisms to operate blinds or draperies. Blinds with continuous-loop cords are easier to adjust than those with pull cords.

OPPOSITE FAR LEFT A ruffled valance is any easy-care choice for a country kitchen.

OPPOSITE LEFT Pleated blinds made from synthetic fabrics are very resistant to mold and mildew, which can feed on natural fibers.

LEFT Protect wooden shutters from soaking up odors and moisture by coating them with glossy paint or varnish.

BELOW Multi-layered window treatments will insulate a bedroom from too much noise or light and are easily adjusted by remote control.

bright idea

test the air

Tape a piece of clean, absorbent, white fabric to a windowsill in the room you're testing. Check it in a week. If it already looks dirty, you need a window treatment that's extremely easy to clean. If not, then leave it, checking weekly to get an idea of how quickly dirt builds up. Note that your window treatments will collect soil more slowly than your test did, because they'll hang vertically and thus shed more of the dirt in the air.

ABOVE LEFT Neutral mid-tones, such as these natural linen blinds, will need less frequent cleaning than white or cream-colored fabrics.

ABOVE RIGHT Woven-wood blinds need only regular dusting to stay fresh and clean.

LEFT Plastic mini-blinds are easy to dust. Wash them with warm, soapy water and rinse.

ABOVE Patterns look clean longer than solid colors do, and weekly vacuuming will postpone the need to dry-clean your draperies.

|||| guard against fading ||||||||||||||||||||||||||||||||

ABOVE LEFT Venetian blinds offer considerable protection from sunlight for printed cotton draperies, even when the slats are open.

ABOVE RIGHT In a very sunny room, consider using unbleached cotton fabric for your draperies. They'll gradually and imperceptibly lighten over time but will look good for many years.

LEFT Bamboo has natural resistance to the sun and is easy to keep clean—an ideal choice for a sunny eat-in kitchen.

Some materials are inherently more durable than others, and some are more susceptible to the ravages of certain elements. Wooden shutters might last several lifetimes in a dry situation, yet warp in a few years in a bathroom where the humidity changes drastically and frequently. Silk draperies could be good for thirty years in a north-facing room, yet crumble into shreds in five years in a sunny window in the same house. It's wise to consider how your material choices relate to durability.

Sun damages all fabrics, fading dyes and weakening the fibers. Many synthetic fabrics, especially those designed for outdoor use, are very sun-resistant, and new technologies have made it possible for them to look virtually indistinguishable from traditional fabrics. Of the natural fibers, linen is most resistant to sun damage, but dyed linen will fade faster than cotton. Silk is very vulnerable to the sun, quickly fading and soon weakening so that it shreds and crumbles. A lining will slow the damaging effects considerably, as will sheer panels or blinds between the window and the drapery.

Sun bleaches the color out of wood (think of driftwood) and dries it, making it brittle. For wooden shutters or blinds, a coat of paint is your best defense. Bamboo is also a good choice in strong sunlight as it has a natural resistance to the damaging rays.

RIGHT Sheer panels are the traditional choice for protecting expensive silk draperies and valuable antiques from sun damage.

guard against humidity

Humidity causes a problem with wood, as it swells and contracts the fibers, causing warping. It also damages the protective coatings—paints and stains—commonly applied to preserve wood. Humidity also attracts mildew, which feeds on paints and natural fabrics, such as cotton, linen, wool, and silk. It rusts and corrodes metals. First, do what you can to reduce humidity with exhaust fans and improved ventilation. Then choose quick-drying plastics or synthetic fabric for window treatments.

ABOVE LEFT A glazed cotton valance is well out of the way of steam from the sink.

LEFT Glossy enamel paint protects wooden shutters from moisture.

ABOVE Polyurethane varnish is less susceptible than paint to the ravages of mildew, making it a good choice for finishing bathroom shutters.

ABOVE A formal dining room is a good place to treat windows with delicate fabrics, such as these silk sheers embossed with a metallic pattern.

frequency of use

This is a big factor in the durability of any window treatment.

▌ A fabric that's handled often will require more frequent cleaning.

▌ Mechanical wear and tear will reduce the lifespan of anything from fabrics to operating mechanisms.

▌ Choose sturdy, well-made treatments for the windows you'll be adjusting daily.

▌ Indulge in delicate fabrics in lightly used rooms.

The amount of money you'll want to invest in your window treatments depends on how permanent you expect them to be. Will you be moving, renovating, or redecorating soon? It may not make sense to heavily invest in treatments with a short lifespan.

On the other hand, if the window treatments are important to your decor and if you expect to enjoy them for a long time, you'll want to spend what it takes to get exactly what you want.

budget considerations

ABOVE Elegant custom blinds represent an investment for this home but would be considerably less pricey for modestly sized windows.

RIGHT Expensive silk fabric and trimming, along with professional design and craftsmanship, went into these draperies.

OPPOSITE These ruched-top draperies and custom fabric blinds were worth the cost; their romantic style makes this bedroom special.

ABOVE Swag a window with a mélange of fabrics and trims to get a luxe look for less.
The yardage required is minimal compared with that for floor-length draperies.

▐▐ what ups the cost? ▐▐▐▐▐▐▐▐▐▐▐▐▐▐▐▐▐▐▐▐▐▐▐▐▐▐▐▐▐▐▐▐▐▐▐▐

materials

TOP LEFT The tasseled fringe on these draperies cost almost as much as the silk fabric.

▐

TOP RIGHT Ready-made panels in durable synthetic fabrics can offer stylish, budget-friendly alternatives to expensive custom work.

▐

ABOVE Handsome poles and finials such as these will increase the cost of dressing your windows.

▐ **Fabric** ranges from a few dollars to hundreds of dollars a yard. Cost has little to do with durability—many expensive fabrics are quite fragile.

▐ **Trims** can cost as much per yard as fabric, and the cost can become considerable as the required yardage increases.

▐ **Lining and interlining,** often necessary to the good looks and proper functioning of draperies, add to their cost.

▐ **Hardware** meant to be seen—poles, finials, and holdbacks—is often pricey. Hidden hardware—rods, brackets, and hooks—is usually reasonably priced.

bright idea

customize for less

Have your dry cleaner hem ready-made panels to the correct length.

construction

▮ **Custom** means that the window treatments are individually designed and made just for you. It is expensive.

▮ **Semicustom** work involves giving measurements and fabrics (which may also be selected from stock) to a retailer who makes the treatment from stock designs. This can be fairly pricey or quite reasonable, especially when you use a large mail-order company.

▮ **Ready-made** window treatments range from cheap to reasonable, depending on the source and the quality. If your windows are standard sizes and shapes, you'll be able to find curtains, draperies, shades, and blinds ready to take home and hang.

▮ **Homemade** window treatments may be the cheapest option if you have the skills. Sewing simple curtains, laminating fabric to a roller shade, and installing ready-made shutters are projects that aren't too difficult or time-consuming.

OPPOSITE It took a professional decorator to design and install these elaborate window dressings.

BELOW Ready-made panels like these are a low-cost way to treat your windows, and they can look great, provided they're full enough and the correct length.

RIGHT Semicustom blinds, shades, and shutters give you a custom look at mass-market pricing.

BELOW RIGHT Sewing your own allows you to have a custom treatment at a great price. If your skills are limited, stick with easy top treatments, such as tabs, rings, or rod pockets, rather than tricky pleated styles.

affordable options

ABOVE It takes little fabric to create a valance; shop for discounted remnants in fabric stores.

RIGHT Generously pleated blinds are a better and cheaper choice than skimpy draperies.

get a chic look for less

There are ways to make inexpensive treatments look like they cost lots more.

- **Hold down costs** by using an expensive fabric for shades, which require less yardage than draperies.

- **Save a fancy fabric** for a valance or cornice to top plain panels or blinds.

- **If you need a lot** of fabric, use burlap or even a bedsheet. Use it generously with plenty of fullness and length, and line it for body and durability.

- **Trim window treatments** with bands of fabric—it's cheaper than fringe, braid, or ribbon.

- **Shop for trimmings** in sewing and fabric outlets or online rather than in stores that specialize in upholstery and decorating fabrics.

ABOVE Fabric bands make an elegant trimming for window treatments and cost far less than ready-made trims without looking like a compromise.

LEFT Consider using a tree branch as a witty substitute for a pole to support your draperies.

RIGHT Inexpensive nylon lace has been given the full-dress treatment of lining, interlining, and pleated heading to make low-cost formal draperies.

spreading the expense over time

layer by layer

Build your window treatment in stages, as you can afford it, and you won't have to compromise on quality.

1 **Begin with a (sheer or opaque) fabric** or wood blind mounted inside the window frame. Alternatively, your first layer could be sheer panels, hung inside the frame and falling to the sill or hung from the top of the frame and falling to the sill or the floor.

2 **Add the drapery panels,** lined (and interlined, if desired) but left untrimmed for now.

3 **Install your top treatment**—upholstered cornice, pleated or gathered valance, swags, jabots, or pelmets.

4 **Add the trims**—fringes, braid, and cording can be easily handstitched in place. Install beautiful holdbacks or concoct stunning tiebacks from remaining fabric and trim.

bright idea

Use and reuse

Hang matchstick blinds to give your living room a finished look while you save for your dream draperies. Later, reuse the blinds in your family room or home office.

OPPOSITE TOP LEFT Pleated fabric blinds will provide light control and give the windows a dressed look while you save up for custom-made draperies.

OPPOSITE TOP RIGHT You could stop with a sheer treatment and panels without anyone being the wiser. Only you have to know that you have future embellishments in mind.

ABOVE Built layer-by-layer, sheer shades, full draperies, and an upholstered cornice, all elegantly detailed, give away no clue that this window treatment was installed over a period of time.

Trim

Frame

Mullion

Trim

Sash

Sill

Apron

ABOVE TOP Inside-mounted fabric blinds require careful measuring to look trim, but they are a good choice for old windows that aren't plumb, because the fabric edges are soft and forgiving of irregularities.

I

ABOVE Use the narrowest width measurement for rigid blinds to be sure they'll operate without scraping against the window frame.

inside mount

Installed inside the window frame, inside-mounted treatments are supported by the frame and cover the sashes but leave the trim exposed. This treatment is commonly used for shades, blinds, and shutters—and occasionally for curtains. Measure:

I The inside width of the frame, from the side of one casing to the other. This is the crucial measurement to ensure a good fit.

I The height of the window from the top of the frame to the sill. A little extra length is not a problem for treatments that are raised and lowered, such as shades and blinds, but is very important for shutters that will cover the entire window.

measuring your windows

What you need to measure depends on what you're installing, but it's wise to have a complete set of measurements for each window; when questions arise, you'll have the numbers ready. For accuracy, always measure with a retractable metal tape. Because windows are rarely perfectly square, take each measurement in three places, choose the shortest, and round up to the nearest ⅛ inch. Refer to the labeled photo, on the opposite page, for the names of window elements.

outside mount

Measuring for outside-mounted treatments needs to be quite accurate for hard materials, such as wooden shutters, which are normally installed on the outer edges of the window trim. Blinds and shades may also be mounted outside the window opening to cover the trim when they are lowered. Measure:

▮ The width of the window from the outer edge of the trim on one side to the other.

▮ The height of the window from the top corner of the trim to the sill. Blinds and shades may be a little longer than this measurement, but shutters must be an exact fit.

TOP RIGHT With an outside-mounted blind you can use a blind that extends slightly beyond the trim if you want the window to appear larger.
▮
RIGHT Shutters should fit a window almost perfectly. They aren't a good option for windows that are badly out of plumb.

standard **l**engths

There are four standard lengths for curtains, and to deviate from them is likely to make your curtains look ill-fitting or strange. Each length carries a message:

▐ **Sill-length.** Just brushing the windowsill, sill-length is the most informal look. Curtains can look perky, sweet, country, or minimalist. They work well in kitchens and baths, in country-, Shaker-, and Craftsman-style interiors.

▐ **Apron-length.** A slightly longer option, it covers the apron below the sill. Tied back, the curtains have an early twentieth-century look (when this length was most popular); left hanging straight, they have a mid-century modern vibe.

▐ **Floor-length.** Actually hemmed to clear the floor by ½ to ¾ inch so that the curtains hang perfectly straight, it is an essentially informal, versatile length suited to either traditional or modern decor.

▐ **Puddled.** Long enough to bunch up on the floor, puddled curtains can either look formal or bohemian. Depending on context, the message can be "I can afford as much fabric as I want," "I used to live in a palace," or "I shop at flea markets." In any case, the effect is romantic.

▮▮▮ measuring for curtains and draperies ▮▮▮▮▮▮▮▮▮▮▮

OPPOSITE TOP LEFT Sill-length café curtains are a classic choice for kitchens. A valance adds country charm.
▮

OPPOSITE TOP RIGHT The timeless look of floor-length draperies makes a serene backdrop for traditional and modern styles.
▮

LEFT Apron-length curtains have a cheerful informality in a bedroom.
▮

ABOVE These puddled draperies are actually one continuous length of fabric that loops around the pole to form the swags.

Fabric treatments allow for a bit more leeway in measuring than do shades, blinds, and shutters. Curtains and draperies can be off by as much as ½ inch lengthwise—and considerably more than that widthwise—and still look fine. Deciding on the length and width of your curtains and draperies is as much an art as a science. Fortunately, there are tried-and-true guidelines to choosing the correct dimensions.

LEFT This heavy silk is lined and interlined to provide the body to hold deep pleats.

BELOW Medium-weight chintz, hung informally from rings, is two and one-half times the width of the window it covers.

BELOW RIGHT These sheer curtains are very crisp; a softer fabric would need to be fuller.

Deciding on the width of curtains and draperies is mostly a matter of correctly evaluating your fabric. Soft, thin fabrics call for more width because they'll hang limply and look skimpy without plenty of fullness. Heavy, stiff fabric will bunch up unattractively if the panels are too wide. Scrunch the fabric in your hand, layered with any lining or interlining you plan to use. Does it compact easily or resist gathering? When draperies are fully open they should drape easily and the pleats or gathers should be dense yet not bunched. The width of the space needed for the proper effect is called "stackback." You need to be sure that there's room on either side of the window for the stackback. When draperies are closed, there should be enough fullness to hang in generous folds.

weight versus width

There are some rules of thumb for determining the width of panels in various fabrics.

▌ **For heavy or stiff fabrics,** such as damask, brocade, many linens, crewel embroideries, and lightweight fabrics that are lined and interlined, use two to two and one-half times the width of the rod.

▌ **For medium-weight fabrics,** such as most decorator fabrics, including chintz and some linens, use two and one-half to three times the width of the rod.

▌ **For lightweight fabrics,** such as gingham and similar cottons, muslin, taffeta, lightweight silks, and polyester sheers, use three to four times the width of the rod.

▌ **For very light and soft fabrics,** such as voile and other sheer cottons, and tissue-weight silks, use up to five times the width of the rod.

bright idea
a look of luxury

Ready-made panels often look cheap simply because they're too narrow. Buy four for each window instead of just two, and get an upscale look without breaking the bank.

width, fullness, and stackback

Everything that supports your window treatment controls its movement, and holds it open or closed falls into the category of hardware. Most hardware is invisible once the window treatment is installed, but it's nevertheless very important—a sagging curtain rod, unable to support the weight of the fabric, is a sad sight. Other hardware is meant to be seen—like jewelry for your window. Shades, blinds, and shutters will come supplied with their own appropriate mounting hardware and controls; it's the fabric treatments that call for careful decision-making.

hardware

ABOVE Standard rods support the swags and jabots at the top of this window, while tension rods are sufficient for the lightweight café curtains.

LEFT A continental rod gives extra body to the heading of this valance.

ABOVE RIGHT Wire rods follow the contours of curved windows, whether they curve in a horizontal plane, as in a bow window, or vertically, as here.

OPPOSITE Most ready-made curtains and valances are designed to use with standard rods.

invisible rods for stationary curtains

Tension rods. These spring-loaded rods slip into a rod pocket stitched into the top of the curtain and slide into the window frame in an inside-mount position. Rubber bumpers cushion the ends of the rod. Tension rods are suitable only for lightweight curtains.

Standard rods. These rods slip into a stitched rod pocket and have curved ends that clip into small brackets mounted onto the window casing. They're available with ends of differ-

ent lengths to hold curtains closer or farther from the window, accommodating multiple layers. They are suitable for medium-weight curtains.

Continental rods. A variation on standard rods, these are extra-wide to add visual interest to the curtain heading.

Wire rod. These are flexible rods that thread through small brackets to accommodate the curves of bow and Palladian windows.

invisible rods for curtains that move

▎**Traverse rod.** This mechanism has runners or a track system onto which pre-gathered or pre-pleated draperies hook. They're easily opened and closed by cords or a battery-operated mechanism, and are sturdy enough to support heavy fabrics. Traverse rods are available with two or three tracks to accommodate multiple layers, and also as a track attached to a plain rod for draperies topped by a stationary valance.

▎**Ceiling-mounted rod.** A variation on a traverse rod, this device is mounted on the ceiling rather than on the wall or window trim.

▎**Swivel rod.** This type of hardware holds the fabric in a stationary position and is hinged on one side to allow the curtain to swing away from the window.

OPPOSITE Draperies that draw need traverse rods. If you use valances with them, install them on a rod that provides enough clearance for the panels underneath to move freely.

BELOW Use a ceiling-mounted traverse rod for a clean look where windows reach or almost reach the ceiling.

BELOW RIGHT A swivel rod lets curtains open and close like a shutter. Be sure to allow for clearance.

poles and finials

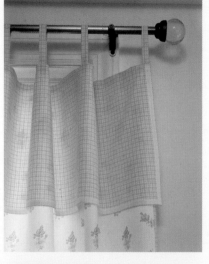

Poles and finials may be wooden or metal and finials may also incorporate glass. Fasten panels to your pole in any of the following ways:

▮ sew-on rings

▮ clip-on rings

▮ a stitched rod pocket

▮ fabric tabs or loops

▮ loops made of cording, braid, or ribbon

LEFT Oversized grommets provide an unusual way to suspend draperies from a pole. Underline the drapery headings for a crisp look.

ABOVE Intricate poles and finials are wonderful additions to a period room, but also consider using them as a surprising touch in a modern decor.

hardware on display

Holdbacks are metal, wood, or glass alternatives to fabric tiebacks. They should match any other visible hardware in material, style, and finish.

Handsome poles, along with finials, rings, and holdbacks can provide an elegant finish to a window treatment. Using beautiful hardware will elevate the simplest draperies to suit a formal setting and can provide a more tailored heading than an elaborate fabric top treatment. Choose a style that expresses the style of your room—from simple wood poles and rings for a country-house look to intricate gilded finials for period-style decor.

custom construction

You are taking advantage of the designer's experience, contacts, and eye for style. You gain access to exclusive "to the trade only" fabrics and trimmings. You are also consuming a great deal of the designer's time, and you should understand that this is a luxury option—not a bargain one.

▮ A designer comes to your home and makes recommendations.

▮ She provides swatches and sketches from which you can choose.

▮ She oversees all measuring, carpentry, sewing, and installation.

ABOVE A designer can ensure that your window treatments are well integrated with the other details of your room.
▮
ABOVE RIGHT This kind of simplicity requires careful workmanship to hang properly and function smoothly.
▮
RIGHT When you're investing in many yards of fabric and trim, it's wise to hire the expertise that will ensure that your window treatment meets your expectations.
▮
OPPOSITE Designers have valuable experience in creating pretty effects with simple means.

If you decide you want professional help with your windows, it's important to do your homework first—not only to find the best value, but also to ensure that you work with someone who'll create the look you want. Get referrals from friends, neighbors, and local retailers. Check local papers and regional magazines for home-design articles and services.

Always ask to see a designer's portfolio; if you like what you see, ask for three references—and be sure to check them. Have pictures from books and magazines of looks you like, ready to show and discuss. Know how much you're willing to spend on the project, and be forthright with that figure. Designers can be creative about using lower-priced

hiring a pro

materials to good effect, but it's better to work with a realistic budget from the beginning of the process.

where to find design advice

When you're not willing to spring for a complete custom package, you can still find help:

▌ Check local home furnishing stores, which often have designers on staff to provide ideas and advice.

▌ Hire a designer on a by-the-hour consulting basis. You'll still have to do the legwork, but she may offer good ideas and may save you from an expensive mistake.

▌ Seamstresses and carpenters, whom you may employ to execute your plans, have often acquired a good sense of design with experience and may know how to achieve the right effect.

bright idea

help is in the mail

Blinds, shutters, shades, curtains, and draperies are all available custom-made by mail-order companies. You measure your windows and choose materials from their stock or send in your own fabric. Find them on the Internet or in home decorating magazines.

OPPOSITE LEFT A good seamstress can create a look like this—especially if you show her a picture.

OPPOSITE RIGHT A bold use of trimming can turn a simple cornice and panels into a unique look.

ABOVE LEFT When creating swagged and draped effects, make a pattern in muslin to check the effect before you commit to expensive fabric.

ABOVE RIGHT You can have draperies like these made by mail-order companies in your choice of fabric.

3

The living and dining rooms are the public face of your home. These "grown-up" spaces are where children learn about company manners and an atmosphere of gracious hospitality prevails. Because the living and dining rooms are not subject to daily wear and tear, practical considerations can often take a backseat to simply creating a beautiful environment. Window treatments are a main component of the decor, helping to set the mood that transports you and your guests from the everyday into a realm that's more refined, stimulating, and glamorous.

Living & Dining Rooms

▮ traditional formality ▮ top treatments ▮
▮ pared-down traditions ▮
▮ modern minimalism ▮

Give a nod to tradition with simplified swags. The sharp black and white stripe gives this window treatment a modern edge.

traditional formality

Window treatments that duplicate period looks have evolved organically from historic needs and desires. Thus, they're multi-layered, both to protect the room from drafts if the windows are old and to shield expensive fabrics from sun damage. They're mounted high and extend to the floor to add height and grandeur to windows that were often smaller, due to economic constraints, than their owners desired. Finally, to display the richness of expensive fabrics and trims, they're elaborately draped, giving full play to the effects of light and shadow.

OPPOSITE Sheer panels shirred on tension rods filter light, while draped swags, pleated jabots, and full-length draperies, all trimmed with tasseled fringe, give these windows the full-dress formal treatment.

ABOVE To tone down the formality, choose gathered valances rather than draped ones.

RIGHT Use casually draped and knotted swags to create a look that's more romantic than formal.

traditional **l**ayers

From the eighteenth, through the nineteenth, and into the twentieth centuries, window treatments were built in layers.

▌ **Sheer or translucent fabrics**—usually cotton muslin, voile, or lace—were made into panels or blinds. Roller shades came into use during the late Victorian period.

▌ **Floor-length panels of rich fabric**, lined, and often trimmed along the inner vertical edges with braid or fringe, were hung from hooks or rings to close over the sheers at night. During the daytime, they were looped back with tiebacks.

▌ **Stationary panels** often—but not always—framed the first two layers. Because they were not meant to move, they were often elaborately trimmed and looped into graceful curves.

▌ **Valances or swags** topped the window, concealing all the underpinnings of the first two or three layers and providing an opportunity to introduce more trimming.

▌ **An architectural cornice** of wood, usually carved and often gilded, provided a strong finish above the valance to top off the fabric layers below.

TOP RIGHT Give the traditional layers an informal look with softly gathered sheer blinds topped by basic panels and a valance.
▌
RIGHT This contemporary take on tradition combines a severely simple fabric cornice with panels and sheers, all in a sophisticated shade of taupe.
▌
OPPOSITE TOP Here, the sheers are swept back and tied high beneath stationary panels draped over curved, uphol-stered matching cornices.
▌
OPPOSITE BOTTOM Use boldly shaped and trimmed cor-nices to formalize casually swept back draperies and fabric-paneled shutters.

Did you know?

curtains and draperies

Historically, "curtains" was the commonly accepted layman's term for any fabric window covering, while "draperies" was the term used by professionals. Today, "curtains" are informal and usually unlined, while "draperies" are formal and lined.

BOTTOM Raising your swag to a point at the center is a good way to make the ceiling look higher.

RIGHT Use traditional window treatments in a sleek setting for an intriguing blend of comfort and glamour.

BOTTOM RIGHT Choose a flat top treatment to give your windows a serene finishing touch. Even with an elaborately shaped edge, the effect is not as busy as a gathered or pleated valance would be.

OPPOSITE Soften your colors and contrasts to tone down a period style.

Whenever you choose to add a top treatment to a window, you instantly evoke a traditional reference, whether or not the rest of the window treatment, or the decor in general, is traditional. For instance, you can take advantage of top treatments to bridge the gap between modern architecture

top treatments

and antique furniture. Using top treatments alone, without the usual accompanying draperies, will introduce a lighter, modern sensibility into a period room.

topper types

The style of a top treatment sets the style of your room:

I **Exposed hardware** in the form of substantial poles, detailed with finials, sets the scene for English country-house style. This look was first popularized in the nineteenth century by English designers.

I **Headings** are the manner in which draperies are attached to their supporting rod. They may be pleated in various ways, ruched, gathered, or padded.

I **Valances** are short fabric treatments—flat, pleated, or gathered—supported by their own rods or poles, which cover the top of the window and the top of any draperies that may hang beneath them.

I **Swags** are short fabric treatments that loop around or drape from a supporting rod to create scallops or festoons. They may incorporate long tails called *jabots*.

I **Cornices** are architectural toppers, made of wood or a wood substitute. They may top draperies or add extra height to the window by topping valances or swags. They may be of exposed wood—carved, painted, stained, or gilded—or padded and upholstered.

LEFT Contrasting bow-tied tapes form a pretty heading.

OPPOSITE BOTTOM A lightly gathered valance is shaped into gentle scallops on the lower edge.

OPPOSITE BOTTOM RIGHT Multiple fabrics and trims are layered into a graceful swag.

BELOW A carved and gilded wooden cornice conceals the top of draperies.

RIGHT Goblet-pleated draperies hang from rings that slide along an exposed pole.

BOTTOM RIGHT An upholstered fabric cornice tops a simple fabric blind.

Many people find somewhat simplified versions of traditional window treatments easier for everyday living; they're less overwhelming, especially in rooms of moderate size. New double-glazed windows are not drafty and modern fabrics are more sun-resistant. Also, today, people prefer lighter, brighter rooms. You can start by cleaning up the first layer, replacing gathered sheers with flat fabric or slatted blinds for a more tailored look. Eliminate unnecessary stationary draperies and elaborate cornices. Choose a simple top treatment, and go easy on the trimmings or forgo them altogether.

pared-down traditions

RIGHT Shutters will serve as well as sheers for a first layer, while panels will make your room cozy without adding much bulk.

TOP LEFT Streamline the look of traditional styles by using colors that pick up the room's paint colors.

ABOVE Use a beautiful top treatment, such as this swag, to gracefully accent your window while allowing due attention to other interesting architectural details.

FAR LEFT Modernize tradition with mini-blinds topped with a flowing fabric treatment that unites swags and panels into one long, seamless window scarf.

LEFT Eliminate the valance to simplify your windows.

use floor-length panels for a sleek look

ABOVE When panels are made of interesting fabric and hang beautifully, there's no necessity for elaboration.

RIGHT If you have beautifully detailed windows like these, use full panels of simple, sumptuous fabric to frame them.

OPPOSITE Try a combination of tailored fabric blinds and silk panels to elegantly unite traditional architecture with modern furnishings.

RIGHT Lighten your windows for summer by removing the draperies and leaving just the top treatment.

▮

BELOW It's easy and inexpensive to change sheers seasonally, from white in summer, shown here, to a rich earthy tone when the weather cools.

▮

OPPOSITE You can use yards of inexpensive gauzy fabric to drape the hardware and frame your windows in summer, while your formal window treatment is in storage.

⫸ lighten up for summer ⫶⫶⫶⫶⫶⫶⫶⫶

I n the days when materials were expensive and labor was cheap, wealthy homeowners had their heavy velvet or brocade draperies removed for the summer to allow for cleaning and to let light and air into the rooms. They protected valuable upholstery with light linen slipcovers. Precious rugs were rolled and stored. All this was a lot of work, and few people today would be interested in following this tradition. But it does set a precedence for using lightly clad windows in a traditional way.

bright idea!

seasonal storage

Take your heavy winter draperies to the dry cleaner in spring to be cleaned and stored, unpressed, for the summer. In fall, have them pressed and pick them up when you're ready to hang them.

polished simplicity

Use well-designed details to give pared-down window treatments a put-together look that suits your formal rooms.

▎ **Sheer panels:** Give them ribbon or braid edgings, interesting headings, or tiebacks that create graceful shapes.

▎ **Fabric blinds:** Embellish with any flat trimmings, including ribbon, braid, and contrasting fabric bands. Choose firm fabrics for crisp pleats or soft ones for draped styles.

▎ **Shutters:** Match the finish to your woodwork for a seamless look, or contrast it to create a focal point. Use decorative hinges for period style or glass knobs for sparkle.

ABOVE RIGHT Perfectly fitted shutters have an architectural elegance that needs no embellishment.

▎

RIGHT Give panels more substance and a dressier look with an edging like this narrow black velvet ribbon. Create a soft drape by hanging them from a row of knobs.

ABOVE LEFT Use tiebacks to shape shirred panels into hourglass shapes. You can alter the proportions by placing them higher or lower; there's no rule you need to follow.

ABOVE MIDDLE Echo another element in your decor—in this case, the pattern on the chair seat—when you plan a trim pattern for your window treatment.

ABOVE Striped fabric bands transform simple fabric blinds into a bold yet dressy treatment.

LEFT Use soft construction to lend a romantic air to minimalist blinds.

RIGHT Dress a window with a draped scarf to make a light frame that is reminiscent of swags and panels.

BOTTOM LEFT Sweep a panel in one direction, a sheer in the opposite, to turn a set of traditional components into an asymmetrical, lighter-looking window dressing.

BOTTOM RIGHT A long window scarf, looped and draped over a pole, is an easy, low-tech way to create a traditional frame for your window without any complicated construction.

OPPOSITE TOP Choose simple swags to inject your room with an air of tradition while maintaining a bright, modern effect.

OPPOSITE BOTTOM Use a broad, contrasting band at the top of your draperies to create the effect of a valance without adding extra bulk.

One of the prettiest and most versatile ideas in modern decor is to pull a form from the vocabulary of classic design, take it out of its formal context, tweak it a bit, and make a statement that's uniquely personal yet rooted in tradition.

An interesting way to lighten and modernize traditional forms is to lose the corset, so to speak. Keep to the historically approved shapes, but relinquish the underpinnings of stiffening buckram, underlinings, and even linings. Let the fabric express its own character, rather than molding it into a pre-designed conformation.

▮▮ eliminate structural underpinnings to soften the look ▮▮▮▮▮▮▮

OPPOSITE Let your fabric drape naturally to make even formal styles and elegant materials look softer and less imposing.

▮

ABOVE LEFT Allow deep pleats to fall as they will, rather than strictly controlling them, to loosen up your room.

▮

ABOVE RIGHT Window scarves are unlined, straight pieces that drape and gather according to the nature of the fabric.

▮

LEFT Lose the heading tape, and leave drapery panels unpleated to give them a soft, simple look.

▮

RIGHT Use a softly draped, tied heading to create a pretty waterfall effect with your panels.

modernize with pared-down details

OPPOSITE TOP Choose plain panels with the single detail of a classically pleated heading to unite modern and traditional styles.

OPPOSITE LEFT Use beautiful hardware and contrasting bands on all the edges to add elegance to a simple drapery.

OPPOSITE RIGHT Understated details, such as this tucked heading, will add a subtle luxury to your window treatment.

ABOVE Handsome hardware may be all the detailing you need to give your windows a finished look.

modern minimalism

Clean, straight lines and simplicity characterize the modern style. But even without the elaborate detailing of traditional styles a modern window treatment can be warm, welcoming, and glamorous. Choose gorgeous fabrics with interesting textures to compensate for the lack of detailing. Or use simple blinds to highlight soaring windows that flood the room with beautiful light. With simple treatments, execution is important; be sure that your draperies are amply full and that the pleats are perfect, because there's nothing to distract the eye from a mistake.

ABOVE Give straight panels generously puddled hems to create a soft flow of fabric around an important window.

RIGHT Sleek fabric panels with rosette appliqués soften shutters without disturbing the serene lines.

OPPOSITE Soften tall contemporary windows with generously proportioned panels that connect them with your furnishings.

I I I I I I I I I use simple treatments for functional coverage I I I I I I I

OPPOSITE **TOP** Matchstick blinds will give you an unobtrusive backdrop for any style or any eclectic blend you wish to create.

OPPOSITE **BOTTOM** Venetian blinds make versatile coverings that suit all but the most formal settings.

ABOVE Floor-length draperies, if hung to draw on rings or traverse rods, can stand alone in any room.

RIGHT Flat fabric blinds provide a softer, but equally neutral, alternative to matchstick or venetian blinds.

use bold styling for contemporary drama

ABOVE Frame a wall of windows with ceiling-hung, puddled draperies for a glamorous focal point.

LEFT Use rich color to take embroidered sheers out of the traditional realm, and to give your windows theatrical flair.

OPPOSITE Blow up dressmaker details, such as banding and shirring, to a grand scale to create unusual, attention-getting window treatments.

RIGHT Embellish an upholstered cornice with raised panels to break up the flat surface.

BELOW Use bands of contrasting tone and texture to add contemporary horizontal accents to your draperies.

use modern embellishments to add detail

Detailing adds interest to sleek, modern window treatments without detracting from the simplicity of the overall effect. Try subtle manipulations of texture and color or unexpected dashes of trimming to add sophistication to the design. For example, trimming the hem or edge of curtain panels in a contrasting color adds interest, but it isn't fussy or elaborate in the way a ruffle or fringe would be. The panels look richer yet they remain tailored and contemporary. Texture is another way to embellish a window treatment. Natural fibers, such as linen, wool, and silk, are all beautiful to the eye and touch.

ABOVE Try a traditional trim in a bright contrasting color to reinforce your color scheme.

LEFT A woven border in your fabric will add eye-catching detail while keeping the smooth lines of your draperies intact.

4

Kitchens and family rooms are the busiest rooms of your home, the spaces where the real day-to-day living takes place—preparing and sharing meals and snacks, catching up on paperwork or homework, enjoying all kinds of home entertainment, working on projects, and even doing the laundry. You'll want these rooms to be warm, welcoming, informal places where family and friends can kick back and truly feel at home. Simple, functional, easy-care window treatments will be most comfortable to live with in these hardworking rooms, but that doesn't mean you can't incorporate charm, style, or even drama.

Kitchens & Family Rooms

I country style I

I contemporary style I

I defining your spaces I

The combination of blue and yellow plaids infuses this bow-trimmed valance with French-country charm.

ABOVE Fruit prints are perfect for a kitchen. Tone down a bold print by using it for valances, combined with plain café curtains, tabbed and banded with a coordinating plaid.

RIGHT Choose wooden shutters for a clean window treatment that lets your table take center stage.

OPPOSITE Use a gathered valance to maximize light from a small bay window. Matching it to the sofa helps unify this relaxed family room.

country style

Country styles remain the all-time most popular choices for kitchens and family rooms—for good reasons. They're comforting because they evoke the past in a gentle, homey, unpretentious way. In kitchens, where food is the focus, country style serves as a reminder of the origins of the ingredients you're using to prepare a favorite family recipe. The materials of country styles are inexpensive and easy to maintain. Simple cottons, such as muslin, gingham, calico, ticking, homespun, and plain linens wash easily and age well, actually looking better over time. Shutters and blinds wipe clean easily and open wide to expel odors and let in fresh air.

LEFT Choose natural linen in softly tailored styles to evoke understated French elegance.

BELOW Use classic chintz in subdued colors to bring English country-house decorum to your kitchen.

icons of country style

Choose from a bounty of international "country" looks, including:

American country. Tied-back curtains in crisp cotton, rustic homespun panels hung from strings rather than rods, wooden venetian blinds with 2-inch slats, ruffled valances topping bare windows

French country. Café curtains, especially in cotton lace, Roman blinds in ticking stripe or toile, neutral-colored homespun linen panels hung from tapes or small rings, fabric roller shades topped with simple tailored valances

English country. Well-washed chintz panels hung by rings from heavy poles, soft fabric blinds in loosely-woven cotton or linen, natural-wood shutters topped by chintz valances, tab-topped curtains in linen or cotton stripes

Mediterranean country. Painted wooden shutters, fabric blinds in bright printed cotton, informally pinned-up translucent cotton panels, simply gathered panels of unbleached cotton gauze

RIGHT Bright prints on dark backgrounds are commonly used on windows in Mediterranean homes to keep rooms cool and shady.

BELOW RIGHT Use unbleached muslin for tied-back curtains to create an iconic American farmhouse look.

American style is warm and welcoming

OPPOSITE TOP Use casually pinned-up panels to suggest Federal-style draperies. Weight the edges of lightweight fabric with heavier bands to help them fall gracefully.

OPPOSITE FAR LEFT These valances have been gathered and tacked up at the top corners of the windows in a Colonial-revival style that was first popular in the early twentieth century.

LEFT Choose a ruffled valance for a cheerful, straightforward look, and hang matchstick blinds beneath to control light.

ABOVE These simple, graceful valances are just straight lengths of fabric, pleated and held by wooden holdbacks.

RIGHT Dressmaker details on this valance, such as the delicate beaded heading, the narrowly piped lower edge, and crisp lining, are hallmarks of French country style.

French country is stylish and charming

LEFT Toile de Jouy, or just toile for short, has been a French classic since the eighteenth century. Use these single-color scenic prints to give a refined informality to your kitchen.

OPPOSITE This dressy but informal kitchen window is worth studying. Identical fabrics used for the valance, jabots, and pleated blind have been worked in exactly the same way on each element of the window treatment, preventing a busy look. Compare this treatment with the similar but simpler one on page 146, which depicts a smaller window in the same room.

let the fabric take you where you want to go

ABOVE Give your family room the exotic air of the Orient with panels of metallic embellished silk. Sari lengths, from Indian import stores or web sites, offer a vast array of colors and patterns.

OPPOSITE TOP LEFT Use a muted tapestry fabric for a valance and blind that will evoke an atmosphere of quiet retreat.

OPPOSITE TOP RIGHT This bold print brings the charm of the Italian countryside to a big-city kitchen.

OPPOSITE BOTTOM LEFT Use printed tablecloths or tea towels from the 1940s to dress your kitchen windows in nostalgia.

OPPOSITE BOTTOM RIGHT A nautical print will bring a beachy mood to your family room—even far from the shore.

ABOVE AND RIGHT
If you have a large space with lots of windows, fabric shades will tie the room together without overwhelming it. These softly draped shades have the jaunty look of a string of banners.

FAR LEFT Use fabric that is the same color and tone of the walls to create flat shades that will provide an unobtrusive backdrop for the room's furnishings.

LEFT Window treatments are one of the few places you can introduce fabric to a kitchen, and a soft shade will often display a dramatic pattern better than a valance or curtain.

BELOW LEFT Generously gathered Austrian shades will give a dressy look to a kitchen and adjoining living spaces, such as this home office, without interfering with countertops.

BELOW False, or stationary, shades or blinds actually function as a valance. Because they won't be moved, you can be creative with your rolling and tying arrangements.

choose fabric shades for versatility

BELOW A flat fabric cornice always looks sleek. Give it a shaped and trimmed edge to evoke a simplified traditional look.

BELOW RIGHT Juxtapose traditional fabric patterns with pared-down styling for a cornice-and-fabric-shade combination that looks modern but not severe.

RIGHT Tailor a traditional chintz pattern into a pleated shade to create a focal point for a glass door, but limit the use of pattern by treating the windows with wooden shutters.

freshening the county look

A too-strict adherence to country conventions can give your room an old-fashioned look you may not want. To update country without sacrificing the charm:

▌ Install a tailored cornice.

▌ Keep fabric valances flat rather than ruffled or draped.

▌ Use solid, neutral fabrics for draped panels or blinds.

▌ Use rolled and tied fabric shades to combine simplicity and softness.

▌ Choose geometric trimmings rather than ruffles and fringes.

ABOVE Try a fabric square draped over a tension rod to create an instant valance. Here, the checked fabric and bows have a country sensibility but the design's simplicity gives this treatment a modern edge.

BELOW LEFT Update an Austrian shade by using a rustic linen fabric rather than the traditional sateen or chintz fabrics.

BELOW An upholstered cornice has modern styling, but the whimsical print on the fabric gives it a countrified air.

pare down formal treatments for a sophisticated look

bright idea

prevent surprises

Wash fabrics in hot water to preshrink them before cutting and sewing your curtains. This will also remove any glazing, which is a telltale sign that a fabric is brand new.

contemporary style

OPPOSITE TOP LEFT Hang flat panels from simple rings on a pole to frame your window in a warm yet modern style.

OPPOSITE TOP RIGHT Use sheer neutral fabric that matches your walls to give a clean contemporary look to a softly looped swag.

OPPOSITE BOTTOM Swag a valance in scallops from wooden holdbacks to make it into a festive flourish that doesn't appear too serious for the kitchen.

ABOVE Choose a subtly colored fabric print for elegant but understated pleated shades.

‖‖‖‖‖‖‖‖ add pretty details to personalize your windows ‖‖‖‖

ABOVE Dress up plain café curtains with contrasting bands and tabs—a great way to enlarge curtains that are a little too small. Add a flat valance in a print that picks up all the other colors.

ABOVE RIGHT Gather a simple curtain on a string instead of a rod to give it a graceful curve and a charming impromptu effect.

RIGHT Cut panels of heavy, glazed paper or translucent acetate; punch holes in the corners; and string them up with ribbon to create a clean-looking, custom treatment that filters light and hides the view.

ABOVE AND LEFT Cut motifs from your drapery fabric, and apply them to roller shades or blinds for a custom match. You can use fabric glue or iron-on fusible webbing to make this a fast no-sew project.

ABOVE AND RIGHT Add interest to your curtain pole by covering it with contrasting fabric. You can stitch a tube to encase the pole or wrap and glue the fabric.

OPPOSITE TOP Shape valances to a shallow point, and attach something interesting, such as these tassels. Crystals, shells, buttons, or beads would work equally well.

OPPOSITE BOTTOM LEFT Dress up a basic matchstick blind by adding narrow fabric bindings to all the edges and a wider fabric heading across the top.

OPPOSITE BOTTOM RIGHT Turn a sheer rectangle of fabric into a versatile, light-filtering window dressing: bind all of the edges with sturdy fabric, and insert grommets every 6 to 8 inches. Hang the panels from cup hooks across the top of the window, and loop up the sides to suit the incoming light.

RIGHT In a multifunctional family room, matchstick blinds will dress the windows functionally without visually intruding on a busy space.

BELOW Use translucent vertical blinds to turn a wall of windows into a clean backdrop for furniture without darkening your space.

OPPOSITE Choose classic venetian blinds to visually unite your breakfast nook with the cabinetry of the adjoining kitchen.

simple windows keep your space serene

defining your spaces

vary **y**our **t**reatments

In a great room—or if your kitchen has a dining table—you may want to signal a transition from the cooking area to the more-formal dining and seating spaces. Window treatments are a great way to simultaneously unite the large space and define separate activity areas.

▎ Dress the kitchen windows simply or not at all.

▎ Use more fabric on windows in the more formal areas.

▎ Match materials throughout, or combine neutral wood or bamboo with fabric.

▎ Carry any trimmings throughout the whole space.

ABOVE Fabric shades with spare but pretty details differentiate the dining area from the working section of this kitchen.

OPPOSITE TOP Use valances to unite all the windows of a large open kitchen, but add floor-length panels to set apart and formalize the dining space.

OPPOSITE BOTTOM LEFT AND RIGHT Scalloped Austrian shades set a dressy note throughout this kitchen, but the dining area benefits from the addition of linen roller shades that provide additional privacy and light control.

unify your great room with valances

ABOVE AND OPPOSITE Where living, dining, and cooking share one large friendly space, valances are the most versatile dressing for uniting a variety of differently sized and shaped windows. Keep your valances uniform throughout, and mount neutral shades or blinds underneath them for light control and privacy.

5

Your bedroom and bath are your retreats from the busy world and the most private rooms in your home. The window treatments you choose for these personal spaces, unlike those for the public and communal spaces in the house, encourage personal expression and foster the pursuit of personal comfort. Create a serene at-home getaway or a romantic fantasy. If you're decorating a child's room, use window treatments to pull together a colorful and creative environment. Keep function in mind, too, with adjustable treatments.

Bedrooms & Baths

❙ comfort ❙ coordination ❙
❙ styles ❙ children's rooms ❙
❙ small bedrooms ❙ baths ❙

Softly tailored linen shades provide privacy and light control in this soothing master bedroom.

Privacy and the exclusion of unwanted light and sound are prime considerations for true comfort in any bedroom, but situations and preferences vary. Begin by assessing your own needs. You may love being awakened by the sun streaming in the windows as the birds tune up—or not. Plan your bedroom window treatments to solve light, noise, and privacy problems and to take advantage of any assets the room affords. For instance, you can use blackout roller shades underneath any other window treatment to completely darken your room while you're sleeping. Lined draperies on a traverse rod will both darken the room and muffle sound. Choose sheer treatments to filter light and provide daytime privacy.

ABOVE Use unlined fabric shades and curtains to soften light but not exclude it.

ABOVE LEFT Venetian blinds provide flexible light control. Drawing the draperies over them will both darken the room and muffle street noise.

ABOVE Sliding fabric panels will filter sunlight where you need it, but they don't offer complete privacy or darkening.

LEFT Venetian blinds topped by lined and interlined draperies will turn your bedroom into a warm, dark, quiet retreat at night.

create a restful room with simple draperies

ABOVE Use pale, neutral tones at the windows to create a quiet backdrop for a restful bedroom.

LEFT Using a rich color for the draperies will make your windows a focal point in a pale room, while limiting pattern and color will ensure a serene effect.

and soft colors ||||||||||||||||||||||||||||||||||||||||||||||||||||

ABOVE A generously ruched heading adds luxurious detail to drapery panels without disturbing the quiet elegance of the room.

RIGHT Match the fabric and trim of your window treatments to that of your bed to create a soothing pulled-together look for the room.

∎∎∎∎∎∎∎∎∎∎∎∎∎ sheer treatments welcome beneficial light ∎∎

ABOVE For the softest look, tone your sheer window treatments to the wall color and drape the fabric loosely.

If your bedroom is a daytime retreat, you'll want to embrace natural light for the feeling of well-being it provides without sacrificing a sense of seclusion. Sheer fabrics offer you the perfect solution. Any sheer treatment can incorporate blackout shades that will provide total privacy and darkness when you want it.

TOP RIGHT Inset a translucent panel into a sheer drapery to increase daytime privacy and filter strong light.

RIGHT Use colored sheers to tint the light that streams in. Here, pale lilac fabric brings a cool cast to the room.

RIGHT Upholster cornices with fabric from an extra sheet to coordinate your windows with your bed linens.

BELOW Use one fabric print for both draperies and bed upholstery, and reinforce the match by trimming the windows and accessorizing the bed with the same accent stripe.

coordination

The prominence of the bed with all its fabric dressing, as well as the cushioning and skirting of other furniture, can unite all of the fabrics in your bedroom into a pleasing, cohesive design, but it will take some planning beforehand. It's important to balance and blend the fabrics at the windows with those used elsewhere in the room to create points of interest and areas where the eye can rest.

bright idea

rule of three

Balance prints easily by following this rule: repeating a pattern in three places in a room generally yields the most pleasing effect.

TOP LEFT Use a coordinated print and stripe to add variety. Using the stripe generously will give the room a crisp, tailored look. Compare this bedroom with the one on the bottom of the opposite page.

LEFT An elaborate print used sparingly in a room of mostly solid colors will command attention.

bright idea
contrast patterned and plain

Showcase patterned fabrics on large areas of solid color to keep your bedroom restful and serene.

RIGHT Trimming plain draperies with a band of fabric that matches a printed coverlet is a simple way to tie a room together.

LEFT Match the finish of your blinds to wood or wicker furniture to subtly coordinate your room.

ABOVE A scarf-like valance of paisley echoes the bed dressings in similar colors without being an exact match.

RIGHT Coordinated fabrics and wallpaper borders offer an easy way to pull together a traditional-looking room.

ABOVE AND LEFT In the bathroom, you can use shades made of the same fabric as your bedroom draperies to unite the two spaces while also differentiating the luxurious quality of the bedroom from the utilitarian nature of the bath. But if the room gets steamy, a fabric treated with mildewcide is more practical.

OPPOSITE TOP LEFT AND RIGHT Use the same fabric as your bedroom draperies, in a scaled-down style, to dress your smaller bathroom windows. Reduce bulk and simplify the trimming to prevent overwhelming the smaller bath with pattern.

OPPOSITE BOTTOM LEFT AND RIGHT Feel free to shorten your window treatments in smaller spaces and rely on identical top treatments to unify the windows.

coordinate your bedroom with your bath

styles

As private refuges, bedrooms offer an opportunity to indulge in decor that's cozy and romantic, whimsical and eccentric, or serene and pampering. Window treatments are more important than any other element in establishing the mood that will nurture your spirit.

ABOVE Soften practical shutters with a sheer fabric panel to provide a gauzy soft backdrop to a feminine dressing table.

ABOVE A gathered silk taffeta shade always lends a romantic air to a room. Choose tailored treatments for the rest of the fabric furnishings to keep the look from going over the top and to allow the window treatment to shine.

RIGHT Turn simple draperies into a romantic window dressing by using a rich silk fabric for extra full and long panels that will puddle on the floor.

RIGHT Glossy satin fabric and an Art Deco-style dia-mond-detailed valance give this window treatment Hol-lywood-style glamour.

|||||||| dress your windows to evoke a simpler time |||||

OPPOSITE TOP Traditional fabrics and shaped, fringed valances evoke Regency-period windows.

OPPOSITE LEFT Combine gingham checks, flowers, and clip-on rings for a country-house window treatment that suits pine furniture and patchwork quilts.

OPPOSITE RIGHT Create Colonial Revival style with blue and white florals, ruffled valances, and scalloped edgings.

ABOVE Graceful draping softens fabric blinds to work with both the straight lines and gentle curves of an eclectic group of antique furnishings.

create a cocoon of soft fabric

ABOVE These window treatments are simply lengths of sheer fabric draped over rods and knotted.

OPPOSITE TOP LEFT Combine gathered shades and panels to provide a gentle backdrop for the bold curves of antique furniture.

OPPOSITE TOP RIGHT Gathered shades dress a window without interfering with the comfort of the adjacent daybed.

OPPOSITE BOTTOM Use an Austrian shade for a voluptuous look without all the bulk of floor-length draperies.

bright idea

fullness without fuss

Choose pale solid colors, small prints, and simple trims to keep feminine gathered treatments pretty, not pretentious. Piling on ruffles and other details can make your treatment cloyingly sweet.

BELOW Make a no-sew valance by draping small square embroidered tablecloths over your drapery rod.

OPPOSITE LEFT With a tension rod and a square of lace you can confect a pretty window topper in just a few minutes.

OPPOSITE RIGHT Layer delicate lace and antique trims in a quiet corner of your bedroom.

OPPOSITE BOTTQM LEFT Bed and table linens that are too fragile to serve their original purposes can be recycled as window dressings. You can hide stained or damaged areas in the folds.

OPPOSITE BOTTOM MIDDLE Inset a piece of lovely old lace into a cotton window panel.

OPPOSITE BOTTOM RIGHT Old monogrammed hand towels can find a new purpose when reconfigured into a valance.

add charm with antique fabrics

ABOVE Edge a simple curtain with a collection of vintage hankies.

ABOVE RIGHT Used another way, hankies with a floral motif look whimsical in combination with a blue-and-white awning stripe fabric.

OPPOSITE TOP Use delicate stenciling to coordinate window, wall, and shower curtain.

RIGHT A roller-shade kit can turn a favorite fabric into a unique window covering.

OPPOSITE LEFT String a few beads onto twine to make a pull cord for a shade.

OPPOSITE RIGHT Customize a simple fabric shade with ribbon edging and a length of beaded fringe.

detail your windows with personal touches

Decorating rooms for your children is an expression of your love and protection, as well as an important way of responding to their individuality. Safety—no dangerous cords—comes first in the nursery. Beyond that, you'll want the windows in kids rooms to provide a bright, pleasant view onto the big world.

children's rooms

LEFT AND ABOVE Valances made up of triangular banners are cheerful treatments for children's windows, framing the view with festivity.

LEFT AND FAR LEFT Simple tied-top panels are sweet for your nursery and will lend themselves to recycling into other decorating schemes as your baby grows. The painted detail on the finials is also easy to change when the time comes.

BELOW LEFT Stitch together a patchwork of baby washcloths for an easy and unusual nursery window.

BELOW Mount a shelf above baby's window from which to hang her cute outfits for a valance-like effect. Even when she outgrows her newborn sizes they'll still serve a purpose.

suit the decor to your child

ABOVE A canoe paddle makes an unusual curtain pole for your happy camper.

ABOVE RIGHT AND RIGHT A pretty valance makes a practical treatment for a child's room. It's well up out of harm's way; it can be easily and cheaply replaced when it's time to redecorate; and you can mount a room-darkening shade underneath to ensure untroubled sleep.

OPPOSITE This elaborate-looking treatment is actually quite practical. The upholstered cornices are easily vacuumed, while the flat curtain panels slip off easily for cleaning.

personalize with cutouts | | | | | | | | | | | | | | | | | | | | | | | | | | | | | | | |

OPPOSITE Customize readymade curtains for your little dress-up artist by gluing on rows of fringe and felt cutouts of shoes and bags.

ABOVE LEFT A small mechanic will love truck designs glued to his window shade.

ABOVE Graphic numbers (from a craft store) and tape measures will thrill your budding mathematician.

LEFT Nurture your preteen's design sensibility with a flower-power window shade.

expand your space

- Match the curtains to the walls for a seamless look.

- Use sill- or apron-length curtains to reduce bulk.

- Install a shade or blind rather than a curtain on a small window.

- Leave any window that doesn't really need covering undressed.

- Match the window fabric to the bed linens.

ABOVE Use a neutral fabric that matches the wall to blend the window treatment into the background and make your room seem larger.

OPPOSITE To indulge in a printed fabric without closing in a small space, choose one with a light background and a single color. Be sure to have plenty of pale, solid surfaces in the room. Here, the walls, bed covering, and carpet all provide relief from the print

C ity apartments, modest homes, and even grand houses have their share of bedrooms that are just large enough to accommodate the bed and not much else. Whether it's a guest room or the only bedroom in the place, you'll want to plan a window treatment that visually expands the space and makes the room look cozy, not confined.

small bedrooms

ABOVE Window treatments that end at the sill leave a clear floor space that accommodates the chair without looking crowded.

ABOVE RIGHT Use a monochromatic print and match the bed to the window to keep a small bedroom from looking overstuffed.

RIGHT Here, the closet curtain matches the walls and the window is dressed with a wooden blind rather than more fabric. A neutral color scheme further enlarges the room.

ABOVE Dress a small, awkwardly placed window simply and distract the eye
with an interesting pattern on the walls and a pretty bed.

Window dressings in your bathrooms must provide all necessary privacy and should be chosen to weather extremes of temperature and humidity. But once those issues have been addressed, the window treatments can be as stylish and fanciful as you like or as simple and functional as you need them to be.

baths

ABOVE LEFT Use an interestingly shaped valance to turn your bathroom window into a focal point.

ABOVE Venetian blinds are a practical solution to bathroom privacy. Add a valance to give the windows a finished look.

LEFT Use valances as decorative treatments in your bathroom. Install shades underneath, and lower them down as needed.

RIGHT Self-adhering vinyl sheets are easily cut to fit glass, give the effect and privacy of etched glass, and are completely unaffected by moisture.

BELOW A roll-up fabric shade can be lowered when needed to cover a French door that opens onto a private deck and garden. If this bath were less sheltered, the translucent fabric would leave this bath too exposed.

BELOW RIGHT Shutters can be opened or closed and the louvers raised or lowered to offer maximum light or complete protection.

no-fuss window treatments serve your needs

LEFT Although there's no view into this bath, the large window feels too exposed after dark. Adjustable shades provide an enclosed feeling when it's desired, allowing the dramatic view inside when they are raised.

BELOW A gathered valance dresses these windows and conceals privacy shades that can be easily lowered when needed.

ABOVE Roman shades introduce fabric without a lot of bulk. They're especially useful for window treatments that need to clear a vanity, countertop, or tub.

▮▮▮ use fabric to add color and pattern ▮▮▮▮▮▮▮▮▮▮▮▮▮▮▮▮▮▮▮▮▮▮

ABOVE LEFT A sill-length curtain can introduce a welcome softness into a room filled with hard surfaces and hard edges. Near tubs and sinks, choose fabrics and styles that launder easily.

▮

ABOVE Try deep valances to bring a dressy note to small bathroom windows.

▮

FAR LEFT Flat-pleated shades display printed fabrics well and don't intrude on space in tight quarters.

▮

LEFT Feel free to use any curtain or drapery style in a roomy bath with full-size windows. It's usually best to hem them to sill level, however, to keep the floor clear.

RIGHT Full gathered shades with contrast pleats, fringed trim, and banded cornices might seem a bit impractical, especially in the wrong setting. But in a large, well-ventilated master bath, well above potential sink splashes and away from the steam of the shower, there's no real reason not to indulge.

BELOW This formal-looking panel is actually just a simply pleated sheer that whisks off for a quick sudsing, drips dry, and is ready to rehang in a few hours.

BELOW RIGHT Dress up basic fabric shades with contrast borders and a beautifully shaped lower edge to bring living room style to your bath.

OPPOSITE Floor-length draperies aren't practical for hardworking bathrooms where floors need frequent mopping, but in a commodious, gently used bath they can be fine, especially if they are easy to remove and clean.

dress your bath with formal styles

IIIIIIIIIIIIIIIII dramatize your bath with special effects III

ABOVE In this large bath with classical leanings, simple sheer window treatments allow the elaborately painted wall murals to define the room.

OPPOSITE TOP Beautifully detailed, gauzy draperies frame an antique vanity in a bathroom designed to evoke an eighteenth-century dressing room.

RIGHT Victorian-style window treatments are just one element of a bath that's a gilded-age period piece of wallpaper, woodwork, prints, and antiques.

Whatever the style, level of formality, or degree of intricacy your window treatment assumes, the details are what will make it polished and complete. Even the most subtle finishing touches—an unobtrusive self-piping, an elegant pleat—will give a simple window treatment an expensive custom look for little effort or cost. Or you can use more lavish trimmings to transform a simple design into a dramatic statement at your windows. For instance, a basic drapery panel can be transformed into something romantic, traditional, or modern, depending on your choice of fabric and trimming.

Designer Details

edgings and bandings ▎ top treatments
blinds and shutters
tiebacks and embellishments

Wide contrast bands add a strong, graphic quality to these draperies, and they pick up the blue accent color that enlivens this serenely neutral living room.

These most versatile trims can be applied to any fabric treatment and may range in importance from a narrow fabric piping or braid, to a flat ribbon or fabric band, or to a long, lush fringe. To keep the look modern, choose flat fabric or ribbon bands, making them as narrow or wide as you wish. Textured braids, ruched or pleated bands, and fringes suit period and traditional styles. Subtle color and texture contrasts look sleek and contemporary, while high-contrast edgings have a traditional look.

edgings and bandings

LEFT Just as a frame helps to separate artwork from the surrounding wall, a narrow ribbon edging can sharpen the edge of printed fabrics.

OPPOSITE TOP Use narrow piping to define the seams where wide windows (or a narrow fabric) necessitate piecing together several widths.

OPPOSITE BOTTOM LEFT Narrow self-piping gives an elegant finished look.

OPPOSITE BOTTOM RIGHT Contrast banding adds interesting detail and definition to simple window treatments.

LEFT When you want to emphasize a gracefully draped edge, a flat-fabric band will do the job without adding any fussy complications.

ABOVE Showcase an intricate narrow textile by using it to finish the lower edge of a pleated blind.

OPPOSITE LEFT Woven braid can add weight, substance, and a pop of color to a lightweight, neutral fabric.

OPPOSITE CENTER Edging one print with another is a great way to tie together different patterns in a room.

OPPOSITE RIGHT Striped fabrics offer many opportunities for contrast without the need for introducing a new material—unless you can't resist adding a cheerful bobble fringe!

RIGHT Use a self-fabric ruffle or pleated edgings to achieve an understated feminine softness.

using edgings

Consider adding an edging to your window treatment when you want to:

▮ Add crispness and definition.

▮ Add weight to a lightweight or soft fabric.

▮ Contain a busy fabric and keep it from overpowering the design.

▮ Differentiate your window treatment from the adjacent walls.

▮ Add either vertical or horizontal emphasis to the windows.

▮ Tie in a color or pattern from elsewhere in the room.

edgings fit into any style

▎▎▎▎▎▎▎▎▎▎▎▎▎▎▎▎▎▎▎▎▎▎▎ fringe softens edges gracefully ▎▎

TOP LEFT Take fringe to the max by weaving an entire curtain from silky ribbons.

TOP MIDDLE LEFT Crystal-beaded fringe will catch the light and do the same thing for your room as a sparkling pair of ear-rings does for a pretty face.

ABOVE LEFT There are plenty of trimmimgs available that are suitable for simple window treatments constructed from humble fabrics. Remember, fringe isn't confined to grand or formal looks.

ABOVE RIGHT Combine fringe with sheer draperies to softly emphasize the edges.

ABOVE Long, silky fringe will define edges in the same way as a fabric band, but with a lighter, more translucent effect.

bright idea

resize with bands

Add length to too-short draperies with inset bands of contrasting fabric and customize them for a new location.

LEFT A wide band of lace enriches these draperies and unifies them with the bed cushions.

BELOW LEFT Use alternating horizontal bands of sheer and opaque fabrics to create a window treatment that reconciles the desire for light with the need for privacy.

BELOW Deep bands of a printed fabric will add a touch of pattern without overwhelming the overall design.

ABOVE LEFT Wide bands of contrasting fabric ground tall windows and relate the windows to the furniture arrangement.

ABOVE RIGHT In a neutral room, changes in tone and texture subtly draws attention to the windows.

RIGHT Even tiny windows benefit from bands. Here, an open texture on the bottom of the curtain admits light while the upper portion shields the view.

Wide fabric bands inset or applied to drapery panels bring a horizontal emphasis, and thus a contemporary edge, to your windows. They're a great way to add detail without a fussy look. Use them for additional color and texture or to coordinate the window treatments with the other fabrics in the room. Inset opaque draperies with sheer bands to lighten the room without sacrificing privacy.

ABOVE Use an extra-deep heading on gathered draperies to create a full, romantic effect.

ABOVE RIGHT Gathers—on the tabs and their bindings—transform a normally tailored heading treatment into something more romantic.

RIGHT Goblet pleats add substance to a simple valance.

top treatments

The headings—the myriad ways that panels can be gathered, pleated, or draped from supporting rods—offer you choices from the dignified to the flirtatious, and everything in between. Use strictly controlled pleats for a formal effect, tabs or rings for a tailored look, or gathers to endow your treatment with feminine charm. Generally, the simpler the heading, the more modern the look will be.

ABOVE You don't need a curtain rod if you can find one in the woods! Using it to hang fringed silk draperies combines the rustic and the refined in a stylish way.

RIGHT Give a simple curtain a perky look by scalloping, binding, and pleating the heading.

RIGHT   A jagged edge gives a Gothic air to the valance, but the window is fixed in the modern world by virtue of its bright, crisp fabrics.

BELOW   Split a valance, and gather it with big self-fabric bows to combine period charm with modern informality.

BOTTOM   Using plate-size rings to scoop up the centers of valances is a bright idea for a dining room or kitchen. These are pewter with fabric-upholstered centers, but the idea lends itself to many interpretations.

top windows with valances for period style

ABOVE Create a romantic valance with short, decorative rods mounted above the windows and draped with sheer fabric.

use cornices as tailored toppers

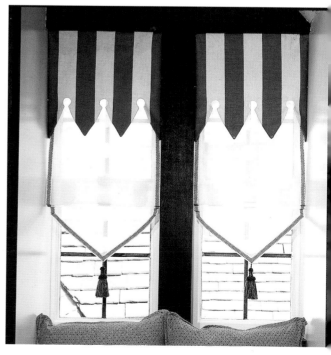

OPPOSITE TOP Boldly shaped and simply upholstered cornices will give your windows an elegant timeless finish—neither distinctly modern nor period in style.

OPPOSITE BOTTOM LEFT Use a wallpaper border on a cornice to get period atmosphere into your room without adding bulk.

OPPOSITE BOTTOM RIGHT The flat surface of a cornice is so easy to embellish. The only tool you need is a hot-glue gun.

ABOVE LEFT Use a shaped cornice to add grace to a wide window and to dress up a simply decorated room.

ABOVE RIGHT A cornice of strong shapes and colors can become a focal point and add a sense of structure to a room with no architectural detail.

RIGHT You can make the most of small windows with elaborately shaped and graphically patterned cornices. Consider oversizing them for a strong impact.

Adding trims to shades and shutters will pull them out of the background and turn them into decorative accents for your room. Your choices range from discreet edgings to bold, colorful effects, depending on whether you want a subtle spot of interest or a focal point in your room. Bind bamboo or matchstick blinds with fabric to dress them up or to coordinate them with your room. Add interest to shutters by antiquing, glazing, or distressing the wood to match the other furnishings.

shades and shutters

ABOVE Edge the pleats of a sheer blind with brocade for a rich, Old World look.

OPPOSITE TOP LEFT An outdoor shutter with an aged patina will frame your windows and bring the garden indoors in a family room, kitchen, or sunroom.

OPPOSITE TOP RIGHT Upgrade a basic roller shade by having it custom-made in quality fabric to highlight a small pretty window.

ABOVE Give your shade a jaunty edge with self-fabric triangles, backed with a contrasting fabric.

ABOVE Use fabric binding to dress up matchstick blinds.

RIGHT A paint treatment creates faux shutters to frame and visually enlarge windows in a dining room.

ABOVE Tying back your curtains needn't be a symmetrical affair—or a once-in-a-lifetime event. Experiment with various levels.

RIGHT Add a summery touch with shells, or express yourself with other treasures. Hot-glue your embellishment to a hook, and hang it over the curtain rod.

FAR RIGHT Details make a difference. Coat a wine cork with glue, and cover it with a spiral of twine to make a pull for a linen shade.

tiebacks and embellishments

Extra decorative touches in the form of tiebacks and other add-ons offer a unique way to personalize your window treatments and express the theme of your decor. You can quickly change the whole look of your room by sweeping back your panels at a different level, adding rich tassels or pretty bows, or adding seasonal references, such as holiday greenery or summery shells. These small details offer a quick and inexpensive way to incorporate a refreshing variety into your window treatments.

ABOVE Tiebacks can be expensive cords and fabulous tassels, or you can get an equally attractive result by braiding some raffia and attaching a few shells.

BELOW Give your own stamp to your window treatments with unusual tiebacks—a Chinese frog, a shell glued to a hook, or a wisp of artificial greenery.

Resource Guide

MANUFACTURERS

Ainsworth Noah & Associates

351 Peachtree Hills Ave., Ste. 518

Atlanta, GA 30305

800-669-3512

www.ainsworth-noah.com

Sells high-quality fabrics and wallcoverings.

Atlas Homewares

326 Mira Loma Ave.

Glendale, CA 91204

800-799-6755

www.atlashomewares.com

Sells decorative hardware. Ideas for unique tiebacks are found on the Web site.

Bed, Bath & Beyond

800-462-3966

www.bedbathandbeyond.com

Sells window treatments and hardware in-store and on-line.

Benartex Incorporated

1460 Broadway, 8th Fl.

New York, NY 10036

212-840-3250

www.benartex.com

Supplies cotton fabric designs from a variety of original collections.

Brewster Wallcovering Co.

67 Pacella Park Dr.

Randolph, MA 02368

800-958-9580

www.brewp.com

Manufactures valances, borders, fabric, and wallpaper in a wide variety of styles and collections.

Calico Corners

203 Gale Lane

Kennitt Square, PA 19348

800-213-6366

www.calicocorners.com

Sells manufactured and custom fabric. In-store services include design consultation and custom window-treatment fabrication.

Comfortex Window Fashions

21 Elm St.

Maplewood, NY 12189

800-843-4151

The following list of manufacturers and associations is meant to be a general guide to additional industry and product-related sources. It is not intended as a listing of products and manufacturers represented by the photographs in this book.

www.comfortex.com

Manufacturers custom window treatments. The product line includes sheer and pleated shades, wood shutters, and blinds.

Country Curtains

At The Red Lion Inn

P. O. Box 955

Stockbridge, MA 01262

800-456-0321

www.countrycurtains.com

Sells ready-made curtains, draperies, shades, blinds, hardware, and accessories, in-store and on-line.

Eisenhart Wallcoverings Company

400 Pine St.

Hanover, PA 17331

800-931-9255

www.eisenhartwallcoverings.com

Manufactures coordinated wallcoverings and fabrics.

F. Schumacher & Co.

939 Third Ave.

New York, NY 10022

212-415-3900

www.fschumacher.com

Manufactures coordinated wallcoverings and fabrics.

Graber Window Fashions

Spring Industries

P. O. Box 70

Fort Mill, SC 29716

800-221-6352

www.springs.com

Manufactures shades, blinds, and window hardware.

Hancock Fabrics

3406 W. Main St.

Tupelo, MS 38801

877-322-7427

www.hancockfabrics.com

Nationwide fabric retailer.

Hunter Douglas, Inc.

2 Park Way

Upper Saddle River, NJ 07458

800-789-0331

www.hunterdouglas.com

Manufactures shades, blinds, and shutters. Its Web site directs you to designers, dealers, and installers.

Resource Guide

Jo-Ann Fabrics and Crafts
2361 Rosecrans Ave., Ste. 360
El Segundo, CA 90245
800-525-4951
www.joann.com
Sells fabrics, notions, patterns, and craft products nationwide.

Kirsch Window Fashions
524 W. Stephenson St.
Freeport, IL 61032
800-538-6567
www.kirsch.com
Manufactures blinds, rods, shades, and holdbacks.

Levolor
4110 Premier Dr.
High Point, NC 27265
800-538-6567
www.levolor.com
Manufactures a variety of blinds, including vertical, wood, and cordless types, as well as cellular shades.

Motif Designs
20 Jones St.
New Rochelle, NY 10802
800-431-2424
www.motif-designs.com
Manufactures a coordinated line of fabrics and wallcoverings.

Plow and Hearth
1107-C Emmet St.
Barracks Rd. Shopping Center
Charlottesville, VA 22903
800-494-7544
www.plowhearth.com
Catalog company that sells insulated curtains, hardware, valances, and sheers.

Portsmouth Drapery Hardware Co.
871 Islington St.
Portsmouth, NH 03801
603-433-4610
www.draperyhardware.com
Manufactures fabrics and easy-to-install window hardware for residential and commercial use.

Scalamandré
300 Trade Zone Dr.
Ronkonkoma, NY 11779
800-932-4361

www.scalamandre.com

Manufactures and imports high-end fabrics and trimmings for the professional interior-design trade.

Seabrook Wallcoverings

1325 Farmville Rd.

Memphis, TN 38122

901-320-3500

www.seabrookwallcoverings.com

Manufactures and distributes coordinated wallcoverings and fabrics.

Smith & Noble

1801 California Ave.

Corona, CA 92881

800-560-0027

www.smithandnoble.com

Catalog company that sells ready-made and semi-custom window treatments, fabric, and hardware.

Southwestern Blind Co.

P. O. Box 10013

Austin, TX 78766

888-792-5463

www.swblind.com

Sells a wide variety of ready-made blinds.

Spiegel

P. O. Box 6105

Rapid City, SD 57709

800-474-5555

www.spiegel.com

Catalog company that sells window treatments, hardware, and related embellishments.

Springs Industries, Inc.

P. O. Box 70

Fort Mill, SC 29716

888-926-7888

www.springs.com

Manufactures window treatments, including blinds and shutters.

Thibaut Wallcoverings

480 Frelinghuysen Ave.

Newark, NJ 07114

973-643-3777

www.thibautdesign.com

Manufactures coordinated wallcoverings and fabrics.

Resource Guide

Waverly

800-423-5881

www.waverly.com

Manufacturers coordinated wallcoverings and fabrics, as well as ready-made curtains and accessories.

York Wallcoverings

750 Linden Ave.

York, PA 17404

717-846-4456

www.yorkwall.com

Manufactures coordinated fabrics, wallpaper, and borders.

ASSOCIATIONS

American Architectural Manufacturers Association

1540 E. Dundee Rd., Ste. 310

Palatine, IL 60067

708-202-1350

www.aamanet.org

An organization of window, door, and skylight manufacturers. The Web site offers a listing of window products and a section on national window safety.

American Sewing Guild

9660 Hillcroft, Ste. 516

Houston, TX 77096

713-729-3000

www.asg.org

A nonprofit organization for people who sew. Members receive discounts for sewing-related materials.

American Society of Interior Designers, Inc. (ASID)

608 Massachusetts Ave., NE

Washington, DC 20002-6006

202-546-3480

www.asid.org

Provides consumers with information about interior-design subjects, including design programs and continuing education. Its Web site offers a designer referral service.

Home Sewing Association

P. O. Box 1312

Monroeville, PA 15146

412-372-5950

www.sewing.org

Provides consumers with project information, press releases, discussions, and sewing-related links.

**Window Covering Association
of America**
3550 McKelvey Rd., Ste. 202C
Bridgeton, MO 63044
888-298-9222
www.wcaa.org
A non-profit trade organization that represents the window-covering industry.

**Window & Door Manufacturer's
Association**
1400 E. Touhy Ave., Ste. 470
Des Plaines, IL 60018
800-223-2301
www.wdma.com
Promotes high-performance standards for windows, skylights, and doors.

Glossary

Apron: Molding installed at the bottom of a window, below the inside sill, or stool.

Austrian Shade: A fabric shade that falls in cascading scallops and is operated with a cord.

Awning Window: A hinged horizontal window that opens outward and is often operated with a crank system.

Balloon Shade: A fabric shade that falls in full blousy folds at the bottom and is operated with a cord.

Bay Window: A multiple-window unit projecting out from the exterior wall of a house, forming an angled recess inside the house.

Bow Window: A large window that is similar to a bay unit, but the recess is curved.

Box Cornice: A hollow cornice of boards and moldings nailed to rafters and lookouts. Also called a "closed cornice."

Box Pleats: Two folds turned toward each other, creating a flat-fronted pleat.

Brackets: Hardware attached to the window to support the curtain rod or pole.

Brocade: A weighty, typically formal fabric in silk, cotton, or wool. It is distinguished by a raised, often floral, design in a jacquard weave.

Buckram: A coarse fabric, stiffened with glue, that is used to give body and shape to curtain headings.

Butterfly Pleat: A pleat with two folds, as opposed to the basic pinch pleat, which has three.

Café Curtains: A window treatment that covers only the bottom portion of a window. Panels are most often hung at the halfway point of the window.

Calico: Lightweight, inexpensive cotton or cotton-blend fabric in brightly colored prints.

Cased Heading: Fabric folded over and anchored with a row of stitching to form a rod pocket.

Casement Window: A hinged

vertical window that opens in or out and is often operated with a crank mechanism.

Cathedral Window: A triangular or trapezoidal window paired with and placed above a large fixed window. The top portion of a cathedral window is often left uncovered.

Chintz: A cotton fabric that is coated with resin to give it a sheen.

Clerestory Window: A window installed near the ceiling.

Cloud Shade: A balloon shade that has a gathered or pleated heading and is operated with a cord.

Combination Rods: Two or three rods sharing one set of brackets. They facilitate the layering of various treatments, such as draperies over sheers.

Cornice: A projecting, decorative box that is installed above a window.

Damask: A jacquard-weave material made of cotton, silk, wool, or a combination with a satin, raised design. Widely used for draperies.

Dormer Window: A window set into the front face of a dormer. A dormer window brings light into the space provided by the dormer.

Double-Hung Window: The most common type, consisting of two sash, one atop the other, which slide up and down to open and close the window.

Draping: A technique of folding, looping, and securing fabric in graceful folds and curves. The drape of a curtain is the way it hangs.

Face Fabric: The main, outer fabric used in a window treatment.

Festoon Shades: A class of adjustable or stationary shades that are made of gathered fabric. Styles include balloon, cloud, and Austrian.

Finials: The decorative ends of a curtain rod or pole.

Flemish Heading: A pleat that is stuffed with batting to create a puffed appearance; also called a "goblet pleat."

French Door: A door, typically with twelve divided panes of glass, used alone or in pairs. It is also used as a fixed window.

Fringe: A decorative trim attached to curtain panels, draperies, top treatments, and other window coverings as an embellishment.

Gingham: A light- to medium-weight, plain-weave fabric yarn dyed and woven to create checks or plaids.

Goblet Pleat: See Flemish Heading.

Heading: The horizontal area at the top of a curtain. Its style determines how a curtain hangs.

Headrail: A boxlike case that extends across the top of a window blind and covers the mechanical devices that operate the blind. Also called a "headbox."

Holdback: Curtain hardware made of metal, wood, or glass. It is installed into the wall or on the window trim and is used in place of a tieback.

Interlining: Made of lightweight, opaque fabric, it is used between the curtain fabric and the lining to add body or to block light.

Jabot: In a swag-and-jabot treatment, it is the vertical element, or tail, which hangs at the side of a sweeping scallop or crescent-shape drape of fabric at the top of a window.

Glossary

Jacquard: A loom, named after its inventor, that uses punched cards to weave intricate raised designs. Brocade and damask are jacquard fabrics.

Jalousie: A horizontally slatted blind or shutter that adjusts to admit light and air and exclude rain and sunlight.

Lambrequin: A painted board or stiffened fabric that surrounds the top and side of a window or a door. Historically, it was also drapery that hung from a shelf, such as a mantel.

Lining: An underlayer of fabric that is added to a curtain for extra body and to filter light and air.

Miter: A sewing technique for creating a flat corner where two hemmed edges of fabric meet.

Moiré: A fabric finish on silk or acetate, intended to resemble water marking.

Mounting Board: A wooden board installed either inside or outside the window frame on which some types of window treatments are attached.

Muntin: Wood trim that sets off smaller panes of glass in a window.

Muslin: A plain-weave cotton; also called "voile."

Pattern Matching: To align a repeating pattern when joining together two pieces of fabric.

Piping: An edging made of cording encased in bias-cut fabric.

Pleated Shades: Shades made of permanently folded paper or fabric.

Pleater Hooks: Metal hooks that are inserted into pleating tape to create pleats in a curtain heading.

Pleating Tape: A cotton or nylon strip, with drawstrings, that is sewn onto the back of the heading to make pleats.

Pole: Metal or wooden hardware that supports curtain or drapery fabric; also called a rod.

Repeat: The duplication of a design motif or pattern at consistent or random intervals in a fabric.

Return: The distance from the front face of a curtain or drapery rod to the wall or surface to which the brackets for the rod are attached.

Rod: See Pole.

Rod-Pocket Curtains: Panels that hang from a rod threaded through a stitched pocket across the top of the panel. This is the most common window treatment.

Roller Shade: A fabric or vinyl shade that is attached to a spring-loaded roller.

Roman Shade: A fabric shade that falls into flat horizontal folds. It is raised by a cord system.

Rouching: Extremely tight gathers used as a decorative top finish to a panel.

Shirred Curtains: Curtains that are gathered on rods at both the top and the bottom of the window.

Stack-Back: The space along the sides of a window taken up by a curtain when it is drawn back.

Swag: A sweeping scallop or crescent-shape drape of fabric at the top of a window. In a swag-and-jabot treatment, it is the center element that is flanked by one or a set of tails (jabots).

Tab-Top Curtains: Panels that hang from a rod via looped fabric tabs.

Taffeta: A silk and acetate weave that appears shiny and maintains

Photo Credits

page 1: Eric Roth page 3: Mark Lohman page 4: Mark Lohman page 6: *top and bottom* Eric Roth; *right* Mark Lohman pages 8-9: Mark Lohman page 10: *top* Mark Lohman; *bottom* Todd Caverly page 11: Mark Lohman page 12: *top* Pizzi + Thompson; *bottom* Your Home UK/Retna Ltd. page 13: *left* Debbie Patterson/Prima UK/Retna Ltd.; *right* Bill Rothschild page 14: *top* Mark Lohman; *bottom* Bill Rothschild page 15: *all* Mark Lohman page 16: Mark Lohman page 17: *top* Paul Johnson, design: Wakefield Interiors; *bottom* Mark Lohman page 18: Alan & Linda Detrick page 19: Walter Chandoha page 20: Mark Lohman page 21: *top* Adrian Briscoe/Country Living UK/Retna Ltd.; *bottom left* Huntley Hedworth/Country Living UK/Retna Ltd.; *bottom right* Mark Lohman page 22: *left* Mark Lohman *right* courtesy of Hunter Douglas Window Fashions. Product shown is from the Applause honeycomb shades collection. page 23: Jessie Walker page 24: Mark Lohman page 25: Mark Lohman page 26: *all* Mark Lohman page 27: Mark Samu page 28: Paul Johnson, design: Austin Interiors page 29: Mark Lohman page 30: Mark Lohman page 31: *top left and bottom* Mark Lohman; *top right* Lucinda Symons/Good Housekeeping UK/Retna Ltd. page 32: *top* Paul Johnson, design: Austin Interiors; *bottom* Todd Caverly page 33: *top left and bottom right* Mark Lohman; *top right* Paul Johnson, design: Wakefield Interiors; *bottom left* Paul Johnson, design: Austin Interiors page 34: *all* Mark Lohman pages 34-35 *top* Paul Johnson, design: Wakefield Interiors page 35: *center* Mark Lohman; *bottom left and right* Paul Johnson, design: Wakefield Interiors page 36: *top and bottom left* Mark Lohman Mark Lohman; *top center* Stewart Grant/Your Home UK/Retna Ltd.; *bottom center* Adrian Briscoe/Country Living UK/Retna Ltd. pages 36-37: Mark Lohman page 37: *right* Jessie Walker page 38: *left top and bottom* Mark Lohman; *right* Tria Giovan page 39: *top* Jessie Walker; *bottom* Mark Lohman page 40: Mark Samu page 41: *top* Pizzi + Thompson; *bottom left* Mark Lohman; *bottom center* Paul Johnson, design: Wakefield Interiors; *bottom right* Tria Giovan page 42: Todd Caverly page 43: *top right* Tria Giovan; *all others* Mark Lohman page 44: Mark Lohman page 45: *left* Mark Samu *right* Mark Lohman pages 46-47: Bill Rothschild page 48: Tony Giammarino/Giammarino & Dworkin page 49: *top* Mark Lohman; *bottom* Tria Giovan pages 50-51: *left and top center* Pizzi + Thompson; *bottom center* Mark Samu; *right* Tria Giovan page 52: Mark Lohman page 53: *top* Tria Giovan *bottom* Mark Lohman page 54: *top* Mark Samu; *bottom* Bill Rothschild page 55: *top left* Mark

Samu; *bottom left* Tria Giovan; *right* Mark Lohman pages 56-57: *left and top right* Mark Samu; *bottom center* Mark Lohman page 58: *top* Mark Lohman; *bottom* Mark Samu page 59: Bill Rothschild page 60: *top* Mark Lohman; *bottom left* Todd Caverly; *bottom right* Tony Giammarino/ Giammarino & Dworkin page 61: *top* Mark Lohman; *bottom* Tony Giammarino/Giammarino & Dworkin page 62: *top* Tony Giammarino/ Giammarino & Dworkin; *bottom* Mark Samu page 63: Mark Lohman page 64: *top left and right* Mark Lohman; *bottom right* Bill Rothschild page 65: Mark Lohman page 66: *all* Mark Lohman page 67: Mark Lohman page 68: *left* Bob Greenspan; *right* Mark Lohman page 69: Mark Samu page 70: Mark Lohman page 71: *all* Mark Lohman page 72: *top left* Jessie Walker; *bottom left* Brad Simmons; *top right* Tony Giammarino/ Giammarino & Dworkin page 72-73: Bill Rothschild page 74: *top* Mark Samu; *bottom* Mark Lohman page 75: Mark Samu page 76: *top left* Adrian Briscoe/Country Living UK/Retna Ltd.; *bottom left* Stewart Grant/Your Hom UK/Retna Ltd.; *center* Todd Caverly page 77: Mark Lohman page 78: *bottom left* Jessie Walker; *top right* Mark Lohman page 79: *top* Brad Simmons; *bottom* Jessie Walker page 80: *left* Brad Simmons; *right* Ken Gutmaker page 81: *top* Mark Lohman; *bottom* Mark Samu page 82: *top left and right* Mark Lohman; *bottom* Bill Rothschild page 83: Mark Lohman page 84: *top left* Todd Caverly; *top right and bottom* Mark Lohman page 85: Mark Lohman page 86: *top left* Tony Giammarino/ Giammarino & Dworkin; *top right* Todd Caverly; *bottom* Mark Lohman page 87: Mark Lohman page 88: *left* courtesy of Hunter Douglas; *right* Mark Lohman page 89: Jessie Walker page 90: Mark Lohman page 91: *all* Tony Giammarino/ Giammarino & Dworkin page 92: Mark Lohman page 93: *top* courtesy of Hunter Douglas; *bottom left and right* Tony Giammarino/Giammarino & Dworkin page 94-95: *top left* Mark Lohman; *top center left and far right* Mark Samu; *top center* Bob Greenspan; *bottom center* Bruce McCandless page 96: *top left* Mark Samu; *top right* Bob Greenspan; *bottom* Mark Lohman page 97: Bill Rothschild page 98: *top left* Tria Giovan; *top right* courtesy of Simonton Windows; *bottom* Pizzi+ Thompson page 99: *top* Tria Giovan; *bottom* Pizzi+Thompson page 100: *top left* Roy Inman; *top right* Nick Carter/Good Housekeeping UK/Retna Ltd.; *bottom* Mark Samu page 101: Paul Johnson, design: Austin Interiors pages 102-103: *left and center* Mark Lohman; *right* Pizzi+ Thompson page 104: *top left* Mark Lohman; *top right* Mark Samu; *bottom* Tony Giammarino

/Giammarino & Dworkin page 105: Mark Lohman page 106: Mark Lohman page 107: *left* Mark Samu; *right* Winfried Heinz/House Beautiful UK/Retna Ltd. page 108: *top left, top right and center left* Bruce McCandless; *top center* Jessie Walker; *center right, bottom left* Mark Samu; *bottom right* Pizzi+Thompson page 109: *top left* Lucinda Symons/House Beautifiul UK/Retna Ltd.; *top right and bottom right* Bill Rothschild; *center left* Bruce McCandless; *center right and bottom left* Tria Giovan page 110: *all* Mark Lohman page 111: *left* Paul Johnson, design: Austin Intriors pages 112-113: *far left and far right* Paul Johnson, design: Austin Interiors; *center left* Bob Greenspan; *center right* Mark Lohman pages 114-115: Bob Greenspan page 116: Mark Lohman page 117: *top* Mark Lohman; *bottom* Tony Giammarino/Giammarino & Dworkin page 118: *top* Mark Lohman; *bottom* Tony Giammarino/ Giammarino & Dworkin page 119: *top* Bill Rothschild; *bottom* Roy Inman page 120: *top* Anne Gummerson; *bottom left* Bill Rothschild; *bottom right* Mark Samu page 121: Mark Samu page 122: *top and bottom left* Mark Samu; *bottom right* Mark Lohman pages 122-123: Mark Samu page 123: *top* Mark Lohman; *bottom left* Jessie Walker; *bottom right* Tony Giammarino/Giammarino & Dworkin page 124: Mark Lohman page 125: *top and bottom left* Jessie Walker; *top right* Tony Giammarino/Giammarino & Dworkin; *bottom right* Tria Giovan page 126: *top* Mark Lohman; *bottom* Tony Giammarino/Giammarino & Dworkin page 127: Mark Samu page 128: *top* Tria Giovan; *bottom* Jessie Walker page 129: Mark Samu page 130: *top* Bruce McCandless; *bottom* Jessie Walker page 131: *top left* Mark Samu; *top center* Bob Greenspan; *top right and bottom* Tony Giammarino/Giammarino & Dworkin page 132: *top* Tony Giammarino/Giammarino & Dworkin; *bottom* Jessie Walker page 133: *top* Mark Samu; *bottom left* Bob Greenspan; *bottom right* Tony Giammarino/Giammarino & Dworkin page 134: Eric Roth page 135: *top left* Mark Lohman; *top and bottom right* Eric Roth; *bottom left* Lizzie Orme/Prima UK/Retna Ltd. page 136: *top and bottom right* Mark Loohman; *bottom left* Bill Rothschild page 137: Mark Lohman page 138: *top* Simon Archer/Prima UK/Retna Ltd.; *bottom* Mark Samu page 139: Mark Samu pages 140-141: *top left* Bob Greenspan; *top center and bottom* Eric Roth; *right* Christl Roehl/Retna Ltd. page 142: *top* Eric Roth; *bottom* Pizzi + Thompson page 143: Mark Samu page 144: *top* Mark Samu; *bottom* Tony Giammarino/Giammarino & Dworkin page 145: *top* Eric Roth; *bottom* Mark Samu pages 146-147: Mark Lohman page 148: *all* Bob Greenspan page 149: Mark Lohman page 150-151: *left* Tria Giovan; *center* Bill Rothschild; *top right* Paul Johnson, design: Austin Interiors; *bottom right* Todd caverly page 152: *top and bottom right* Mark Lohman; *bottom left* Tria Giovan page 153: Mark Lohman page 154: *bottom left* Mark Lohman; *top right* Eric Roth page 155: Mark Lohman page 156: Mark Lohman page 157: *top left* Tria Giovan; *top right* Bill Rothschild; *bottom left* Tony Giammarino/Giammarino & Dworkin; *bottom right* Mark Lohman pages 158-159: *top and bottom left, top center and bottom right* Bob Greenspan; *bottom center* Mark Lohman; *top right* Eric Roth page 160: *bottom left* Bob Greenspan; *bottom right* Tony Giammarino/Giammarino & Dworkin page 161: *top left* Mark Lohman; *top right* Bob Greenspan; *bottom left and right* Tony Giammarino/Giammarino & Dworkin page 162: *top left* Tria Giovan; *top right* Mark Lohman; *bottom* Mark Samu page 163: Tria Giovan page 164: *top left* Bob Greenspan; *top right* Brad Simmons; *bottom* Bruce McCandless page 165: *all* Bob Greenspan page 166: *all* Tony Giammarino/Giammarino & Dworkin page 167: *top* Bob Greenspan; *bottom left* Mark Lohman; *bottom right* Tria Giovan page 168: *all* Mark Lohman page 169: Bill Rothschild page 170: Ann Gummerson page 171: *top* Jessie Walker; *bottom left and right* Mark Samu pages 172-173: Mark Lohman pages 174-175: Tria Giovan page 176: Mark Lohman page 177: *top left* Tria Giovan; top right Pizzi+Thompson; bottom Eric Roth page 178: *top* Bob Greenspan; *bottom* Eric Roth page 179: *top* Jessie Walker, design: Marsha Jones; *bottom* Eric Roth page 180: Bob Greenspan page 181: *top* Mark Samu; *bottom* Bob Greenspan page 182: *top* Bob Greenspan; *bottom* Tony Giammarino/ Giammarino & Dworkin page 183: *top* Bob Greenspan; *bottom* Eric Roth page 184: *top* Oliver Gorden/Prima UK/Retna Ltd.; *bottom* Ann Gummerson page 185: *top* Eric Roth; *bottom* Pizzi+Thompson page 186: *all* Eric Roth page 187: *top* Mark Lohman; *bottom* Pizzi+Thompson pages 188-189: *left and top center* Eric Roth; *bottom center* Tria Giovan; *right* Jessie Walker page 190: *top* Pizzi+Thompson; *bottom left* Bob Greenspan; *bottom right* Bill Rothschild page 191: Tony Giammarino/Giammarino & Dworkin page 192: Pizzi+Thompson page 193: *top left* Mark Samu; *top right* Tria Giovan; *bottom* Tony Giammarino/Giammarino & Dworkin page 194: Bob Greenspan page 195: *top left* Bruce McCandless; *top right* Eric Roth; *bottom left* Christopher Drake/Country Living UK/Retna Ltd.; *bottom center* Brad Simmons; *bottom right* Caroline Arber/Country Living UK/Retna Ltd. pages 196-197: *top left and right* Bob Greenspan; *top center* Jessie Walker; *bottom left* Emma Lee/Country Living UK/Retna Ltd.; *bottom center* Simon Whitmore/Best UK/Retna Ltd., *bottom right* Adrian Briscoe/Country Living UK/Retna Ltd. page 198: *top* Pizzi+Thompson; *bottom* Tony Giammarino/Giammarino & Dworkin page 199: *top and bottom left* Bob Greenspan; *bottom right* Mark Lohman page 200: *top left* Bruce McCandless; *top right* Jessie Walker; *bottom* Tony Giammarino/Giammarino & Dworkin page 201: Eric Roth page 202: Bob Greenspan page 203: *all* Bob Greenspan page 204: Mark Lohman page 205: Mark Lohman page 206: *all* Tria Giovan page 207: Mark Samu page 208: *top left* Tria Giovan; *top right* Bob Greenspan; *bottom* Pizzi+Thompson page 209: Ann Gummerson pages 210-211: *top left* Bruce McCandless; *top right* Mark Lohman; *bottom left* Pizzi+Thompson; *bottom center* Tony Giammarino/Giammarino & Dworkin; *bottom right* Tria Giovan page 212: Eric Roth page 213: *top left* Eric Roth; *top and bottom right* Mark Samu; *bottom left* Mark Lohman page 214: *top and bottom right* Mark Lohman; *bottom left* Bob Greenspan page 215: Tria Giovan page 216: Mark Samu page 217: *all* Mark Lohman pages 218-219: Mark Samu page 220: Mark Samu page 221: *top* Mark Samu; *bottom left* Mark Lohman; *bottom right* Sarie Visi/Camera Press/Retna Ltd. page 222: *left* Mark Samu; *right* Tony Giammarino/Giammarino & Dworkin page 223: *top* Mark Lohman; *bottom left* C. Gratwicke/Country Living UK/Retna Ltd.; *bottom center* Tony Giammarino/Giammarino & Dworkin; *bottom right* Bruce McCandless page 224: *top and center left* Mark Samu Mark; *bottom left* Bruce McCandless; *right* Mark Lohman, design: Judy Taylor Interior Design page 225: Jessie Walker page 226: *top* Mark Samu; *bottom left* Tony Giammarino/Giammarino & Dworkin *bottom right* Lizzie Orme/Good Housekeeping UK/Retna Ltd. page 227: *top left and right* Eric Roth; *bottom* James Merrell/Country Living UK/Retna Ltd. pages 228-229: *top left and bottom right* Mark Samu; *all others* Jessie Walker page 230: *top left* Mark Samu; *top right* Tony Giammarino/Giammarino & Dworkin; *bottom* Roy Inman page 231: Bill Rothschild page 232: *top left* Bill Rothschild; *top right* Tony Giammarino/ Giammarino & Dworkin; *bottom left* Eric Roth; *bottom right* Bob Greenspan page 233: *top* Tony Giammarino/Giammarino & Dworkin; *bottom* Ken Gutmaker page 234: *all* Tony Giammarino/ Giammarino & Dworkin page 235: *top left* Mark Samu; *top right* Todd Caverly; *bottom left and right* Mark Lohman page 236: *top* Jessie Walker; *bottom left* Bruce McCandless; bottom *right* Graeme Ainscough/House Beautiful UK/Retna Ltd. page 237: *top left, bottom center, bottom right* Bruce McCandless; *top center* Tony Giammarino/ Giammarino & Dworkin; *top right* Jessie Walker; *bottom left* Mark Samu page 243: Roy Inman page 244: Mark Lohman page 247: Eric Roth page 253: Mark Samu page 255: Mark Samu

If you like
Design Ideas for Windows,
take a look at the rest of the
Design Idea series

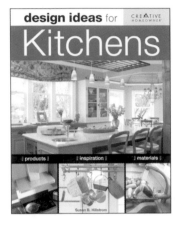
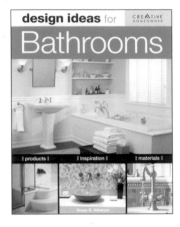
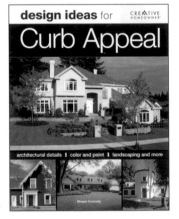
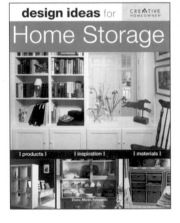